Jonathan Gledhill, Bishop of Southampton, has spent over 20 years working in different kinds of parish, as well as teaching such subjects as New Testament, mission and preaching to ministers-in-training. He is married and has two grown-up children.

Being a personal prayer means coming from han an encounter with God, having heard from him recently, having renewed our own relnshp w him

Sware
releases gift
HS p17
Ps 24,25
M 32 testg · nec pol of munch

Leading a Local Church
in the Age of the Spirit

Jonathan Gledhill

Published in Great Britain in 2003 by
Society for Promoting Christian Knowledge
Holy Trinity Church
Marylebone Road
London NW1 4DU

British Library Cataloguing-in-Publication Data

A catalogue record for this book is available from the British Library

ISBN 0–281–05471–1

1 3 5 7 9 10 8 6 4 2

Typeset by Pioneer Associates, Perthshire
Printed in Great Britain by
Antony Rowe Ltd, Chippenham, Wilts

For Jane,
la migliore fabbra

Contents

viii   *Contents*

Preface

I was watching a sailing boat on a lake. The scenery was magnificent, there was a fine sailing wind, but the crew were obviously inexperienced and the sails were flapping noisily. They struggled and the boat drifted slowly backwards. It is amazing how quickly a sail can wear out when left to beat itself against the shrouds. Suddenly it all came right: either they backed the jib or twitched the rudder or, more likely, there was a wind-shift. At any rate they were sailing; the painful flapping changed into the surge of foam at the bow, and even from the bank I could sense the power as the boat heeled gracefully, and rushed away from me.

These chapters come out of the experience of being at the helm when things have gone wrong – and when they have gone right. Often it has not been exactly clear what caused the flap or what happened to make it go right again, but now and then it has been clear, and the resulting sensation of powering up has been so exciting that I had to write about it.

My thanks go to the people of All Saints, Marple, and St Paul's, Strines, in Greater Manchester; St George's and Holy Trinity, Folkestone; St Mary Bredin and Wincheap, Canterbury; for their friendship and patience over many years. In some sense they are the anonymous co-authors. Although the anecdotes are all true, some details have been changed to protect privacy. Thanks also are due to my good friends Mike Booker, Stephen Cottrell and George Lings for reading the first draft, as well as to Mrs Liz Marsh of SPCK for her encouragement and editorial work.

I
Being a Leader

A DAY IN THE LIFE

An early call comes this Monday morning from the labour ward of the local hospital: it is the chaplain's day off and a mother has given birth to twins; one has died and the other is in intensive care. I drop everything and go. The staff nurse fills me in on the details: the mother came in the day before; her waters had broken early; they tried to keep the babies from being born too soon, but failed. She takes me in to see the mother and father, and their little wizened first-born, smartly dressed in a white bonnet in the incubator – but stiff and cold. His name is Austin.

The parents want to discuss funeral arrangements; should the burial be here at the hospital where the authorities have just marked out a special plot for neonatal deaths, or back home at Folkestone? Then the young mother asks about baptism for her dead baby. I suggest anointing instead and we all gather round little Austin – parents, grandparents, uncle and myself – and anoint the tiny stiff head, praying:

> *Almighty God, you make nothing in vain, and love all that you have made. Comfort this woman and her husband in their sorrow, and console them by the knowledge of your unfailing love; through Jesus Christ our Lord.[1]*

We pray for the tiny twin still fighting for life in the ward above and I discover that the family knows Psalm 23 by heart as well as the Lord's Prayer. There are faith and courage in this ward as well as sadness, I reflect on the way home, and there will be much to pass on to the chaplain as she prepares the family for the funeral.

This morning is staff meeting morning. The 'staff meeting' consists of the two clergy, a Reader, two pastoral assistants and the administrator. It is not good for humans to be alone, and building teams is a useful way to make and be disciples. We begin with Morning Prayer and then pray for one another. The student worker is struggling today with his feelings in the face of the demands that people make on him; it is not easy to manage an apparently unstructured timetable. So we gather round to pray for him in particular. Then we study the next chapter of a book over coffee; as minds and hearts grow together through thinking and praying, so we learn to act together. Next we go back over the past week and pick up points and pastoral concerns. Yesterday we had a Seekers' Service[2] *with a particular focus on enquirers and so spend some time debriefing. Opinions are sharply divided about the effectiveness of a 'seeker-friendly' service. Then we outline our responsibilities for the week ahead. Normally we end at twelve, but occasionally we have an extended staff meeting to look further ahead, so today we raise our sights and make plans for the next quarter. Finally we have a simple lunch together and plan a summer outing. Holding together this talented team of people with such different experience and character is a delight – and challenging.*

In the afternoon I have a meeting with the new diocesan surveyor and a builder; it is time for the inspection of the vicarage which takes place every five years, and we go round kicking drainpipes and examining electrical fittings. I wonder if I have aged in five years as much as the external woodwork on the house.

The answer is probably 'yes', I decide, as one of the pastoral assistants and I take session two of the Youth Alpha course in a room full of excitable teenagers on their way home from school. 'How do you know that God is there?' asks one lad. 'Surely it is not fair that Jesus should die for other people's sins?' and so on. We love the knockabout discussions with no pulled punches.

There is time for a cup of tea with my wife Jane and for some paperwork before an engaged couple arrives to discuss wedding arrangements. As I spent some time last week with two people wanting to end their marriage, I find the seriousness and enthusiasm of this couple encouraging.

After supper some of the church leaders arrive for an evening of discussing and praying together with us. The PCC is too large for much creative thinking and so from time to time I gather this smaller

group of wardens, Readers and one or two others, to think creatively
and take time to listen to God.

They leave at ten and Jane and I put our feet up, have a drink
together and discuss all that has happened to us both before making
our way to bed.

SHEEP AND SHEPHERDS

Christian leadership – lay or ordained – depends on a series of
relationships. When Jesus said, 'I am the good shepherd', and
'Feed my sheep . . . Follow me',[3] we think we understand what he
was saying, but in fact the metaphor needs some unpacking.

Down on the farm, sheep do not grow into shepherds. They
may learn things from following the shepherd and having their
ankles nipped by the sheepdog, but they are never asked to take
over the flock. With the Church, however, things are more complicated – and more exciting. At one moment a Christian leader is
required to take authority or initiative – faced, for instance, with a
request to baptize a dead baby. At another one finds oneself in a
servant role, putting away chairs or listening attentively to someone's opinion that one has often heard before; at another in a
partnership or co-ordinating role, waiting to make sure that a
decision is a team effort. At yet another one's part is to receive and
be ministered to. The roles and relationships keep changing – and
necessarily so.

Jesus himself is seen in the New Testament as both the Good
Shepherd and the Lamb of God. He is sheep and shepherd. To the
first generation of Christians the meaning of each of those terms
was clear: 'shepherds' was a way of referring to leaders in general
and to the Lord God as leader of his people in particular; 'sheep'
referred to the people. So Psalm 100.3 says, 'Know that the LORD
is God! . . . we are his people, and the sheep of his pasture.'
Ezekiel 34.2 is a condemnation of the nation's leaders for neglect-
ing the first duties of leadership: 'Thus says the Lord GOD: Ho,
shepherds of Israel who have been feeding yourselves! Should not
shepherds feed the sheep?' These and other familiar texts are
taken up and reinterpreted by Jesus in the Gospels.

When Jesus chose his first followers, the twelve, they were initially to be his sheep, part of his flock.[4] Just as God was the Shepherd of Israel,[5] the leader of the nation, so the twelve, the founder members of the New Israel, were to see Jesus as their Good Shepherd, the leader of God's new family. Their discipleship was first of all a learning to live in relationship with him.[6] Part of that learning was watching Jesus in his relationship with his heavenly Father, his prayer life, his dependence, his discerning what the Father was requiring, and finally his obedience 'unto death'. By being their shepherd, Jesus was also modelling for them, demonstrating to them, what it means to be a sheep.

Of course in the Old Testament sheep were also used for the sacrifices that played a key part in the relationship between God and his people. It is one of the paradoxes of our redemption that the most 'shepherdly' thing that Christ has done for us, namely dying on the cross, was also the most 'sheeply'.[7] The shepherd becomes 'the Lamb who was slain';[8] our great high priest becomes the sacrificial victim. So in John's Gospel Jesus is introduced as the sacrificial 'Lamb of God' who will take away the sin of the world and declares himself to be the Good Shepherd who lays down his life for the sheep.[9] For the early Church, 'lamb' was a highly nuanced reference back to the Old Testament sacrificial system and to Jesus' vocation as sacrifice and scapegoat which would culminate on the cross. Here is deep mystery: that God's great heart of love demands that Abraham be willing to sacrifice his only son, that God's own people fail to be his people, and that life and ministry emerge out of death and sacrifice. The supreme good news – that the apparent defeat of the Messiah is the moment of glory and victory, in fact the turning point of human history – fills the pages of the New Testament and inspires the martyrs.[10]

It is out of this paradox that the disciples learnt to be the first church leaders. Just as Jesus lived powerfully out of his relationship with the Father and the Spirit, so the apostles were nourished by their relationship with Jesus, first as sheep, and then as undershepherds. The Holy Spirit turns sheep into shepherds (and then into sacrificial lambs). It is exciting to read in the book of the Acts how, after the martyrdom of Stephen, the gospel is spread by the anonymous disciples; and how some of those delegated to do the catering, like Philip, become vigorous evangelists, with the clear expectation that their converts will also in time convert others. Even Paul, the great apostle to the Gentiles, knows that the church in Rome was planted not by apostles but by those unknown Christians who have been grasped by the Spirit and the Good News.[11] Sheep have the potential to become shepherds.

One of the key differences between the Old Testament and the New is that whereas in the Old the Holy Spirit fell upon certain individuals – kings, prophets, heroes – to equip them for particular ministry, in the New he is promised to 'all flesh'.[12] The Church has not always understood this. For centuries the expectation in a pastorally orientated and settled Church in the West has been the essentially Old Testament expectation that sheep remain respectfully sheep and pastors remain pastors. This has led to a disastrous weakness in the modelling or demonstrating of the truth. In the typical Anglican church when people become Christians they look round for someone to help them in their new life, but there are few if any lay models. They see the vicar, who may well be their first point of contact with the church; unconsciously the thought comes that to be a 'real Christian' is to be ordained. Why? Because this is the most visible model of a Christian that is to hand. Where lay modelling is typically rare, the sheep struggle. A nurse showed me some embroidery she had done for her parish church. With a wry smile she related how she had been fêted and praised for her 'work' by her church for the first time in her life; no one had said anything for the previous 25 years when she had been in charge of a busy ward and struggling daily with issues of life and death. There were many times when she would have valued some prayer and discussion about what it meant to be a Christian on that ward. She wanted to be shown what it might mean to be a Christian leader at her place of work.

Modelling is vital for Christian growth and ministry. In my theological college I learned a great deal in theory about how to be an ordained minister. But the most powerful model available to us there was that of the accomplished academic lecturer. There were good tutors but only a few had experience of leading churches. For three years we sat and drank in this model. The lecturers may have been *talking* about church history or doctrine, but what they were *living* and what was being modelled to us was how to be a good lecturer in a theological college.

So how can this dynamic of 'sheep-into-shepherds' take place? Three things that the worldwide charismatic renewal has helped the Church to rediscover are:

1 Every Christian, however humble, has the Spirit, is a witness and therefore in some sense a potential leader, even if it is only (only?) in leading one other person to Christ. The letters to the churches in Revelation 2—3 for instance assume, like all the Johannine writings of the New Testament, that leadership comes first of all from suffering and serving, not from power or position.

2 Every Christian leader, of whatever rank or status, can only continue to lead effectively through the ongoing experience of being led. If King David wrote Psalm 23, I like to think of him writing it out of the experience of the burdens of office and leadership. St Paul wrote that he would speak only of what God was doing through him.[13]

3 Leadership in the Church is corporate, elastic, flexible. So much of the anguish over the ordination of women would have been avoided if we could have seen the pastoral/presbyteral role in the Church as essentially a matter of teamwork.

This is not to pretend that 'every member ministry' can mean a congregational free-for-all without authority or structure. On the contrary, the more that every member exercises his or her ministries the more a congregation discovers its need for wise leadership. Equally parish priests or pastors gain in authority when they can train others, release gifts, and make converts who will become leaders in their turn.

Of course this makes for a looser and more organic kind of leadership. In an exploding situation where communities are welcomed, new Christians are being made, gifts are being discovered and ministries commissioned, there will be growth, many trainee ministers and not a few mistakes.

TRUE LEADERSHIP

A prominent leader of one of the New Churches has a provocaʳ quip that goes, 'You are not a leader unless someone is following you.' He is right to point out that authority in leadership is not the same as status; there is a weakness in those denominational structures which appoint people to leadership structures first and hope that people will follow them afterwards. But the Gospels are more uncomfortably radical than this. Jesus' teaching on leadership could be summed up as 'You are not a leader unless someone is being served by you.'[14]

This was not only the teaching of Jesus but also the way that he modelled leadership for his apostles. It is significant that John's Gospel contains no record of the Last Supper (though its language is the most eucharistic of all the Gospels). Why is the Last Supper omitted in John? Some scholars believe that the status of the president at the Eucharist was already a matter of conflict when John was gathering his material and that the inclusion of the footwashing in the upper room in John 13 rather than the institution of the Lord's Supper is a deliberately sharp comment on squabbles over the status of presidency.[15]

In this famous episode God in his love glorifies his Son by overturning our expectations about status. In particular there are three things which clearly scandalize traditional notions of leadership. The first is what we might call 'divine disorder'. Verse 1 is full of order and calm and the fulfilling of plans: 'Now before the feast of the Passover, when Jesus knew that his hour had come to depart out of this world to the Father, having loved his own who were in the world, he loved them to the end.'

But in the fourth verse Jesus 'laid aside his garments' (in an echo of the kenotic laying aside of his glory),[16] and 'girded himself with a towel', before proceeding to wash the disciples' feet. It is at this point that fundamental disorder enters the scene. When the guest of honour at the dinner becomes the waiter, when the chairman of the board takes on the role of office cleaner, or when the cathedral dean becomes the verger, received notions of decency and order break down. Jesus is not only saying that to bring about our salvation the Son of God will leave the throne of the universe to be the slave, but that leadership in his Church is to follow that same reversal of the expected order. We still have a weak reminder of this in the Maundy money ceremony in the UK where the sovereign used to wash people's feet in a symbolic way but now presents deserving pensioners with specially minted Maundy coins. But we do not seem to have such a reminder in our church leadership ceremonial. Ordinations and inductions might be more powerful if clergy were presented with a towel and bowl as a sign that we take seriously the Lord's command.[17]

The second thing in this episode that runs counter to our traditions of church leadership is what might be termed 'anti-hierarchy'. It is to the shame of the Christian Church that 'hierarchy' both as a word and as a concept is linked to priesthood and ecclesiastical history. The printing and widespread dissemination of the Bible was one of the key elements in leading Europe towards ideas of commonwealth and democracy from the seventeenth century onwards.[18] But in practice, it has to be admitted, large sections of the European Churches have always supported the *anciens régimes* and fought tooth and nail to protect their own privileges, against the obvious intentions of their Founder.

The third thing which has struck me forcibly in recent years, is what might be called the 'intimacy' that the foot-washing episode records. On Maundy Thursday in our own church we have sometimes attempted to wash people's feet, but this has always seemed a precious and self-indulgent gesture, with little point in a culture where people wear socks and tights. Far better (I had assumed) to encourage those who wish to do something useful on Maundy Thursday to help by putting out the chairs or by washing up the coffee cups. But I had failed to see, until a woman colleague pointed it out, that to wash someone's feet is not only a useful and humbling task, but also an intimate one. Perhaps the nearest we come in our culture to touching one another in such a way is to help people in and out of their coats when they call on us. To make coffee or put out chairs is undoubtedly useful, but it is not intimate and – as I now see – loses one of the essential resonances of this episode.

When Jesus solemnly tells his friends and future leaders of the Church that they are to love one another as he has loved them, he is (among other things) commissioning them to see that leadership in the Church and in eucharistic meetings of the Church is to be characterized by that same godly reversing of the 'natural' order, hierarchy and holding-at-a-distance, in order that a powerful demonstration of intimate and humble servant-leadership may take place.

ST PETER – A REAL LEADER

The Trinity in orthodox theology is often depicted as a kind of community dance. Each Person in the one Godhead has a different role to play, and each moves in and out of leading and being led, of loving and being loved. Sometimes the Spirit leads the Son into the wilderness and the Son submits; sometimes the Son breathes out the Spirit and the Spirit glorifies the Son. This is not only mysterious but also a pointer to good human leadership. For leadership to work well the leader has to be part of a team in which, even if he or she has an overall responsibility, other department heads and people with particular giftings or roles will be given authority to exercise them and the 'overall' leader will frequently find himself or herself in the position of being led and of receiving ministry.

St Peter's role in the New Testament is helpful here. He is clearly seen as the leader-in-training in the Gospels and the *primus inter pares* in the Acts and Epistles. It is he who in the foot-washing episode learns that before he can be of use to Jesus he must allow Jesus to do things for him. Leadership in the Church is not about us making our mark in history but about us being marked by God, and marked in such a way that we can be of service. This is what we see in the career of Peter. It is one of the remarkable features of the New Testament documents that they present such an unflattering portrait of the apostles. It is too easy to explain this (as some form critics have done) merely as the result of different factions in the early Church producing rival versions of their arguments. It is much more likely and more consistent with the teaching of Jesus that what we have modelled for us here is leaders who are vulnerable, fallible and, crucially, still learning.

So, long after Pentecost, Peter is depicted in the Galatian

correspondence as being obviously wrong about the foundations of the faith.[19] The same point is put more positively in his learning experience before the visit of Cornelius.[20] In the Gospels the portrait is even starker. There are many unflattering things recorded about Peter but none more serious than his boasting of loyalty followed by the threefold denial of Jesus; a denial moreover of a kind that the Gospel warns can have eternal consequences.[21] If Peter is in some way representative of Christian leaders then this is a clear-sighted estimate of our limitations. Although the sacrifice of Christ challenges us to attempt to love sacrificially it is plain that we can never be a sacrifice for sin and that we can never be more than under-shepherds. The beautiful recommissioning of Peter at the lakeside not only models the sensitive rehabilitation of the apostle. It also and significantly reports Jesus as prophesying that Peter will be led at the end of his ministry rather than leading, reminding all of us that our strength and tenure of office are fragile and short-lived.[22]

Perhaps the most extraordinary contrast of all, however, comes in Matthew 16. Matthew is the Gospel that emphasizes Peter's leadership role, and in this chapter Jesus gives Peter the keys to the kingdom. But immediately afterwards Jesus says to Peter, who has tried to steer him away from talk of his arrest and death, 'Get behind me, Satan! You are a hindrance to me; for you are not on the side of God, but of men.'[23]

This is an interesting study of the risks of delegating authority! Roman Catholics have naturally interpreted the handing on of authority in a way that legitimizes the authority of the institutional Church and the Bishop of Rome. Protestants emphasize the authority of the revelation that has been given to Peter and see the Church built on that word which proclaims Jesus as Son of God. Each interpretation captures part of what Jesus is saying but both ignore the central thrust of his words. Jesus is obviously not talking about an institutional authority or one vested in an office; equally obviously he is not bypassing Peter and building on words alone – however precious.[24] He is saying that he will build his Church on those people, exemplified by Peter, who are being changed by the power of God. So Peter, the naturally unstable, is given a new name and identity as 'the Rock Man'. Is this a New

Testament running joke, a triumph of hope over experience, or is it a promise that Christ will build his Church through people being transformed by the Spirit?

This nuanced approach to human leadership in the New Testament has many practical implications for the modern Church. For instance the structures of the Methodist Church where people move in and out of being chairman of the Methodist Conference seem to have more of the radical bite of the gospel about them than Anglican and Catholic structures where you inherit a palace for life! I have never understood why cathedral canons and archdeacons do not move back into parish work and wonder whether it might not be good for bishops too. But it is at local church level where leadership sclerosis becomes most obvious to ordinary worshippers. The vicar who has been there for a decade and more and still has to lead and direct everything himself is no longer a traveller. The same is true of housegroup or youth group leaders. Something within them has died if there are no Timothies being trained up in the congregation.

The thesis of this book is that each local church is called to be not only an outcrop of the Church universal but also a training ground of the Spirit, in which lost sheep are found and sheep become shepherds and in which shepherds learn all over again what it is to be a sheep, sometimes to the point of 'For your sake we are being killed all day long'.[25]

The words 'leader' and 'leadership' may not be prominent in the New Testament but the concepts are certainly there. The metaphor of discipleship as a walk or pilgrimage presupposes someone who will guide and lead. When the Epistle to the Hebrews talks of Christ as the pioneer of the faith, and tells us to strengthen our weak knees, it assumes that to be a disciple is to follow in Christ's footsteps, and to encourage us the Spirit has left human leaders for us to follow on the way.

Good leadership is essential in any congregation, as all church-wardens know. It is not a concept to shy away from. Just because the word 'leader' has unfortunate associations it does not mean that Christians can dispense with it. We have to think about leader-ship in the way that Jesus and the apostles taught and modelled it. It would be ironic if, at a time when industry and commerce have become increasingly convinced of the importance of 'servant-leadership', the Church were to be less clear in its thinking about this subject.[26] There will always be something of the now and not yet about human leadership. It will always be derivative, more illustrative of what is wrong with human nature than of what is right with Christ's. And yet, however dimly, we are called to reflect the glory of Christ, and the promise is that God will keep on working away at us, polishing up the reflection.[27]

LIVING OUT OF THE RELATIONSHIP

To be a leader in the Church of God is a calling first of all to be a person of prayer. This is obvious even at the most functional level. How can we lead the worship of the people of God if we do not come fresh from the presence of God? How can we speak his word if we have not been hearing from him lately? How can we build a community of love if we are not constantly renewing our acquaintance with Love? How can we help others to a mature faith if we are not practised in intercession?

But that would be to put the cart before the horse, as functional approaches to ministry have a way of doing. The reality is quite the other way round: the Hound of Heaven has chased us, the Lion has grasped us as his prey.[28] We have discovered that to be truly human is to have a desire for God, to have a passion to know him better. And then of course, when we have been touched by the divine Love, we cannot keep the Good News to ourselves: 'Woe to me if I preach not the gospel.' Out of the over-abundance of God's goodness we receive strength to serve; from the fire of God's love there is fire in our belly; from the ever-deepening water of life flowing from the altar in the temple there is a well of water for the healing of the nations.

Or that is how it is on good days. On bad days it is different: we turn to God in despair at the recalcitrance of our human nature, in anger at the way in which he appears to be mismanaging the world, in anguish at the pain all around us and disappointment that we have failed again. All of these have always been an important part of praying, as evidenced in both Testaments and the lives of all the saints.

The greater problem occurs, however, on those days which are neither particularly good nor bad, but on which the heavens seem closed, the Bible is boring, our spiritual routines irrelevant, and we find our minds wandering towards practical solutions to our problems. If God is on holiday this week, we find ourselves saying in effect, then we will proceed without him.

When H. P. Liddon, the great nineteenth-century preacher and vice-principal of Cuddesdon College, Oxford, spoke at the anniversary festival of the college in 1868 on the work and prospects of theological colleges,[29] he chose as his text these famous words from Isaiah:

> The Lord GOD has given me the tongue of those who are taught, that I may know how to sustain with a word him that is weary. Morning by morning he wakens, he wakens my ear to hear as those who are taught. The Lord GOD has opened my ear, and I was not rebellious.[30]

Liddon, the gentle scholar and future Professor of Exegesis at Oxford, used this verse to speak out against the drily critical and over-academic approaches of his day to the ministry. The cynic, he said, can never hear the voice of Christ speaking, as he reads. But the faithful parish priest who prays daily for his parish will find God speaking powerfully as he reads the daily offices.

Christ himself, maintains Liddon, is the model of the 'tongue that is taught'. He had an ever-open ear to the voice of the Father; he regularly rose before dawn to be alone with him, and it was out of that time that he was able to minister to others. Indeed so evident was this connection that the disciples begged him to teach them to pray. They themselves would have been taught how to pray in their own families and at the local synagogue, but this relationship of Father to Son struck them as something new that must be learned.

Therefore, Liddon concludes, there are few verses of Scripture that furnish so appropriate a motto to be graven over the gateway of a theological college:

> So, still, as of old, morning by morning, in the church of God,

the ears of Christ's ambassadors are wakened to listen to new applications of His once-for-all given message of mercy, or of new and unsuspected treasures contained within the vast storehouse of His healing Truth.[31]

This is why Anglican clergy are given a set pattern within which to grow their prayer life. There are several different alternative structures, from the old Book of Common Prayer to the latest prayers and readings on the Internet, but all are rooted in the ordered praying of the synagogue, based on the Scriptures, and have been tried and tested through the centuries. To many it may seem strange that words as structured as the Daily Office and the Lectionary of the Church can be the vehicle of passionate and intimate prayer. But we are such frail creatures that some kind of objective structure is necessary if our devotions are not to be driven by the vagaries of our emotional states.

Of course the offices of morning and evening prayer are only a structure. They provide a framework into which can be built opportunities for singing, silence, exercising spiritual gifts, inter-cessions and simply enjoying God's presence. They provide a rhythm not only for the day and for the week but for the seasons and moods of our lives, so that we learn to lie fallow as well as to sprout in our praying, to sow as well as to reap.

Over the years those who use the Office find the systematic reading of Scripture plus the discipline of praise, confession, listening and intercession, dedication and recommissioning, a foundation for a life of responsive listening to God. It is true that the way in which we are drawn to prayer is in part a matter of temperament. Some of us are more naturally contemplatives. Extroverts find it easier to pray with others than alone. But these differences, important though they are, should not mask the fact that the quietening and disciplining of the inner self is a struggle for all of us. Sometimes praying is like attempting to teach a class of hyperactive five-year-olds – anything and everything distract from the task. Sometimes it is like trying to control a wild monster – our imagination goes in all the wrong directions. The offices are a gift to disciples who are still being trained by the Spirit.

As soon as I was able to start building a staff team I made it our practice to pray one of the offices together and to use the other for personal praying. The young pastoral assistants who join us for a year have initially experienced this way of praying with incredulity and a conviction that they will find it boring and irrelevant. One complained about the undue wear on the knees of his trousers. But later in the year they come to the patterned time of corporate prayer with increasing understanding and appreciation; several have come back years later to give thanks for a pattern that has served them well in their different lives.

PRAYING THE WEEK

It was Gordon MacDonald in his seminal little book *Ordering Your Private World*[32] who pointed out that time flows from what we find difficult to what we find easy. 'Unseized time flows towards my weaknesses.' In other words if I find it easier to tidy my desk than to prepare a sermon then I will frequently find myself tidying my desk and leaving preparing my sermons until the last moment. Similarly because prayer is difficult I will find myself skimping on praying and doing all sorts of other and more immediate but ultimately less important tasks than praying. It was of bishops that it was well said, 'When it comes to a choice between prayer and work, work will always win, because it is easier.'[33]

Strangely, however, devoting myself to the tasks of the week does not make me more efficient. It is a human characteristic to fill time with tasks, and church leaders find themselves over-busy. Even secular management studies often recommend a period of quiet recollection at the beginning of the day so that the tasks can be properly ordered. Many a general has spoken of the difference it makes to have an overview of the terrain before battle begins. Professional sportsmen and women learn to prepare for a match by thinking through their part in it in advance. Christians find that tasks done after contact has been consciously renewed with their Leader will be done better.

Because of the tendency of my mind to wander during prayers to the tasks of the day ahead, I used to keep a rigid separation between prayer times and work. When a hymn or a reading reminded me of someone I had failed to visit, for instance, I would quickly write down the name on a scrap of paper and return to the prayers – or lose concentration completely. In recent years however, in my desire to make the doing of the tasks of the day part of my response to God's grace, even part of my worship, I have tried to be more active during my praying in laying the week before God and asking for his mind on the activity ahead. I started to try to listen to God's voice, principally through the lections for the day, and hear from him about the needs of the week ahead.

PRAYING IN THE SPIRIT

Human life is lived in the gap between what we know and what we do not know. I know, for instance, how old I am, but not how long I will live on this earth. It is striking that Christ himself, who seemed to have so much supernatural knowledge, spoke also of his ignorance about the future.[34] For if he knew everything how could he have demonstrated faith?

Similarly it is hardly surprising that St Paul is recorded as speaking not only of his knowledge but also of his ignorance. For example in Acts 20, in the moving account of Paul's last meeting with the Ephesian elders, there is a curious, repeated emphasis on what they do and do not know. In verse 18 Paul says, 'You yourselves know how I lived among you all the time from the first day that I set foot in Asia' and in verse 34 he says, 'You yourselves know that these [bare] hands ministered to my necessities.' The apostle is appealing to their shared experience and memories. Before we learn to know facts we know people,[35] and the models of prayer in the New Testament demonstrate that knowing is supremely about spending time learning to know a Person. Which is why Jesus came to live among us, and why the gospel must always be incarnate in people before it can be grasped as proclamation.

The second kind of knowing is to know those things that Paul taught the Ephesians during his three years among them.[36] He did not hold anything back but explained 'the whole counsel of God'. This kind of knowing too is open to us all and builds Christian community.

Then, Paul also says, there are things that he does not know. In Acts 20.22 he says, 'And now, behold, I am going to Jerusalem, bound in the Spirit, not knowing what shall befall me there.' Even the great St Paul lived a life full of uncertainty. Even a cursory reading of the Acts of the Apostles shows that the early Church was subject to the same kind of chaotic uncertainty that we experience. The Holy Spirit did not tell Paul the exact purpose of his journey to Jerusalem or whether the imprisonment was going to start then or later – indeed the whole book of the Acts ends on uncertainty. We can say that Paul and the Ephesians did know one another well, they did know the good news of Jesus, but there were all sorts of things they – like us – did not know.

Into this uncertainty comes a third sort of knowing: Holy Spirit knowing, prophetic knowing. In Acts 20.23 we are told that Paul knows through the Holy Spirit that imprisonment and troubles are waiting for him; in verse 25 that 'I know that . . . you . . . will see my face no more'; and in verse 29, 'I know that after my departure fierce wolves will come in among you, not sparing the flock.' How did he know? Was it just guesswork? It might have been; there was no certainty. And there have been Christians who have claimed to know things but who have been quite deluded.

However, it is the record of Scripture that the early Church expected disciples to live by this kind of knowledge as well as by personal knowing and knowledge of the gospel. Paul and Barnabas were set apart for their mission by a revelation of the Holy Spirit. Paul was guided by the Spirit, did miracles by the Spirit; and the Church was built up by the Spirit. This has been true through the ages: the missionary pattern is that as you pray, something of God rubs off on you, something of the good news is burned into you, and the Holy Spirit reveals parts of the task to you. This encourages you to go, to press on, take risks and then, often, to see wonderful signs accompanying the proclamation of the gospel.

It is an area of ministry where there are no experts,[37] and any prophetic words need careful evaluating.[38] However, it is an essential part of being a church leader to grow in this kind of knowing as well as the others. Otherwise there is little cutting edge to our preaching and no sense of direction in the strategy. I am weak in this area and am encouraged by colleagues who are more sensitive

2
The Age of the Spirit

UNION AND COMMUNION

The Lord is here.
His Spirit is with us.[1]

What makes Christians is our relationship with Christ. Like the ancient Israelites we know that it is only in God's going with us that we are in any way distinct.[2] How is his going with us, his presence among us, known? The traditional Orthodox and Catholic answer to that question would emphasize the liturgy, the Eucharist and the apostolic succession of ordained ministers; the traditional Protestant answer would emphasize the word of God, his promise and the covenant. Both those answers are important, but both also require those emphases to become part of people's experience before they can be passed on. As Lesslie Newbigin, one of the great missionary bishops of the twentieth century, said in his ground-breaking book *The Household of God*, there is a third great stream of the Christian Church, largely neglected by theologians in his day, to put alongside the Catholic/Orthodox and Protestant streams. This is the Pentecostal or charismatic stream:

> Its central element is the conviction that the Christian life is a matter of the experienced power and presence of the Holy Spirit today... If we would answer the question 'Where is the Church?', we must ask 'Where is the Holy Spirit recognisably present with power?'[3]

A colleague of mine, a quiet and faithful high-church priest of many years' experience, who was rector of one of the largest multi-parish benefices in the diocese, had a charismatic experience in which the lordship of Christ became more real to him than ever before. He wrote a letter to his bishop: 'Dear Bishop, I write to tell you that I am no longer in charge of the parishes of A, B and C. Jesus is!' The bishop dropped everything and rushed round to see him, fearing he had had some kind of breakdown!

Several years later, now that this man has moved to another parish, any fair-minded observer would report that:

- though there have been problems, the village church where this spiritual renewal first started has grown and flourished, and the whole village has been touched by it;
- in particular lay leadership has been the engine of this growth;
- there was no question of a breakdown; rather a strengthening and a building-up;
- renewal has also affected the man's new parish.

According to Newbigin, we had become accustomed in the modern Church to discussing the Holy Spirit as a doctrine. But in the New Testament the presence of the Holy Spirit appears rather as a sheer fact.[4] 'By this we know that he abides in us, by the Spirit that he has given us.'[5] Jesus came to change his people's relationship with God for ever by the giving of the Spirit. What in the Old Testament was the experience of a few outstanding people like Moses and David was, as the prophets foretold, to be part of the birthright of all Christians. The New Testament era is the Age of the Spirit when through Christ every believer can call God 'Our Father'.

LIVING WATER

This is made explicit in John's Gospel where Jesus interrupts the climax of the Feast of Tabernacles in Jerusalem. The great feast lasted for several days and was associated with harvest and with the nourishing of old Israel in the desert. Part of the ritual was the pouring out of a pitcher of water over the altar in anticipation of the outpouring of the Spirit in the last days. At the climax of the feast Jesus cried out,

'Let anyone who is thirsty come to me, and let the one who believes in me drink. As the scripture has said, "Out of the believer's heart shall flow rivers of living water.'" Now he said this about the Spirit, which believers in him were to receive.[6]

There is in fact no direct Old Testament citation here, but the Old Testament is full of the use of water as a symbol for our relationship with God and of thirst as a metaphor for spiritual longings. Jeremiah, for instance, has the Lord complaining that his people 'have forsaken me, the fountain of living water'.[7] Perhaps the most striking passage, though, is where the prophet Ezekiel speaks of the time when the living water of God will flow out from a renewed altar in Jerusalem and flood the land with healing for the nations.[8] It is difficult not to see Jesus here, interrupting the festival, as setting himself up as the new altar of God from which the water of the Spirit would flow. The old temple was being declared obsolete and the new temple is the relationship of disciples with Jesus which enables us, like him, to call out 'Abba, Father'.[9]

The Church has grown and developed over 2,000 years not primarily because of a succession of bishops nor because of the spread of Bibles, but because this relationship with the Father, through Christ, in the Spirit, is one that can be experienced by any believer and passed on in every generation. The living water is truly living, and Christian leadership enables people of all sorts and conditions to drink.

FROM PENTECOSTALS TO CHARISMATICS

Into the spiritual drought of the early twentieth-century West the Pentecostal movement burst forth, with the Azusa Street outpouring in Los Angeles in 1906. Under the leadership of William Seymour, a black bishop, the worship and praise in the Spirit went on in the Azusa Street chapel for weeks, laying the foundations for the most rapid spread of the Christian faith since the time of the apostles. The key features of the spiritual outpouring were, first, the speaking in tongues, the prophesying and the experience of being baptized in the Spirit and, second, the coming together of white people and black people under black leadership. Next year a Pentecostal revival broke out in the Anglican parish of Monkwearmouth, Sunderland and was said by the vicar,

Alexander Body, to have continued for some years.[10] It is marked by an inscription on the wall of the church hall: 'September 1907: WHEN THE FIRE OF THE LORD FELL IT BURNED UP THE DEBT.'

What have become known as the phenomena of Pentecostalism were not of course completely new. While the spiritual experiences of ordinary Christians and congregations go largely unreported, the exceptional and miraculous are clearly present throughout the Christian centuries. Justin Martyr, Irenaeus and Tertullian assume the existence of the spiritual gifts and ministries in the Church in the first three centuries. The desert fathers have their ecstasies and battles with demons. St Augustine of Hippo reports divine healings and other miracles too many for him to detail. Gregorian chants are connected with singing in tongues and indeed Pope Gregory the Great writes his *Dialogues* about miracles and prophecies. Francis of Assisi had a well-known healing ministry. Thomas Aquinas has an experience of God in comparison with which all the writings of his great *Summa* appear as 'straw'. Luther and Calvin both testify to God's supernatural power at work in their lives. Ignatius Loyola writes about the spiritual gifts and ministries in his *Spiritual Exercises*. Blaise Pascal sews into his jacket a reminder of the time when the Pentecostal fire fell upon him. The Age of Reason sees the great revivals, and the nineteenth century has the holiness movements and camp meetings. Missionary biographies speak of being filled with the Spirit on the long journeys to the mission field. All these prepared for the outpouring of the 'third stream'. What the New Testament leads us to expect in the realm of experience is present one way or another in all the Christian centuries.

It would be good to report that the amazing growth of the Pentecostal churches was welcomed by the mainline denominations in England in the first half of the twentieth century, but it was not, and particularly not by the Anglican Church. Much more scandalous was the lack of welcome given by the churches to the Caribbean workers recruited by the British government after the Second World War. The reconciliation of black people and white people at Azusa Street did not happen in the UK. When the

Windrush brought hundreds of black immigrants to Southampton in 1948, many of them were devout Anglicans and made their way on their first Sunday to churches in the city. At church after church, they and their children report, wardens and clergy – not recognizing that the gift of the Holy Spirit was for 'all flesh'[11] – told them that they would be better to join the Pentecostal churches. So they did – or started their own charismatic fellowships. In 1998 at the fiftieth anniversary of the coming of the *Windrush* and her sister ships, heartfelt apologies were given to black communities by the churches, but it was sobering to see that those inner-city church buildings which in the 1950s had turned away the newcomers had now nearly all closed. It is a kind of parable of the way in which major denominations can miss the signs of what God is offering us. And yet, by God's mercy, some of the good things rediscovered by the Pentecostals did start to touch the older denominations too, and what we now call 'charismatic renewal' brought about a renewed 'age of the Spirit'. But, with some honourable exceptions, it was a movement from the grass roots.

In 1963, that heady year when J. F. Kennedy died and when the Beatles became famous, two books were published in the UK that have since become symbols of two quite different movements in the Christian Church. The first was *Honest to God* by John Robinson,[12] then Bishop of Woolwich, which popularized the 'radical theology' of Bultmann and Tillich and tried to 'demythologize' the gospel by stripping away those supernatural aspects of the stories that were deemed no longer believable by moderns. The other was *The Cross and the Switchblade* by David Wilkerson,[13] an American pastor whose dramatic story about his discovery of the miraculous in the Christian faith introduced the charismatic movement to the UK for many.

Who would have guessed in 1963 that 40 years later such a large proportion of ordinands and clergy seeking new posts in the Church of England would describe themselves as having been touched by charismatic renewal? Or, by contrast, how dated the 'demythologizing' enterprise of *Honest to God* now seems?

UNITY AND DIVERSITY

One of the skills that church leaders find they have to acquire is how to nourish spiritual growth without losing unity. New initiatives require wise oversight. In each of the passages in the New Testament that teaches about spiritual gifts, there is an emphasis on the Holy Spirit as the agent of both unity and diversity in the local church. Because the Day of Pentecost is a kind of reversal of the curse of Babel, the Church experiences the Holy Spirit as the One who, in the worship of the Messiah, unites the warring tribes.

So, for instance, in Ephesians 4, St Paul (whom I take on the best evidence to be the author[14]) teaches about what makes a church work as it should.[15] The first part of the chapter (verses 1–6) is about maintaining the unity of the Spirit. Christians are to be enthusiastic about being part of a community that depends on the reconciliation of very different people-groups. As Paul suffers a loss of freedom in prison, so he urges on his converts that they have been called to a similar loss of individual choice in order to live together in love and harmony.

One of the key challenges of church leaders is to persuade strong characters that to fulfil their calling they must give up some of their own private agendas for the common good. I remember arriving at a parish where there were thriving housegroups, each of which had its distinctive theology and separate programme. To persuade the undoubtedly gifted group leaders that God might want some part of their programme to be in common with the other emerging housegroups was no small task; asking one of them to write the programme for the whole church was part of the means!

The same Holy Spirit who produces unity and fellowship also gives a wonderful diversity of gifts.[16] The range and variety needed to be the Church go far beyond the New Testament lists, which are plainly a small selection rather than a complete catalogue. But neither should these gifts, listed in Romans 12, 1 Corinthians 12, Ephesians 4 and touched on elsewhere, be excluded from the modern Church, awkwardly though some of them sit with our world views and social organization. I have never forgotten the excitement of discovering 1 Corinthians 12.7, with its insistence that every Christian is given some open demonstration of the Spirit for the common good. Here is empowerment indeed!

It is part of the privilege and challenge of Christian leadership to help people first to discover and then to use their gifts. It is part of the responsibility of a church's leadership to use spiritual gifts in such a way as to encourage others to see gifts and talents as a means of building up the whole church. A common pattern in church life is for untidy growth to take place and for a new minister to have to rein in or even close down a congregation or an organization that has started to become too independent. Pruning is, of course, an important part of growth, but spiritual unity is not the same as tidiness, and judging in practice how to encourage diversity that will not become anarchy requires the wisdom of Solomon.

Ephesians 4 has a very different style of church life in mind from ours, and lively churches often learn much from it. Only five gifts are picked out in this chapter, but they are foundational for the growth of the church because they are the ministry gifts, which enable the community to function. They also challenge our stereotype of a church where there are clergy, who are paid to minister in a building, and lay people who pay them to do so. In Ephesians 4 by contrast is a list of gifts that no one person's talents can encompass: apostles, prophets, evangelists, pastors and teachers.[17] According to St Paul, if the Christians in a local church are to be equipped for their lives of service in the world, then these five gifts are going to be present in the ministry of the church.[18]

APOSTLES

The original generation of apostles were the twelve and the one or two others chosen and authorized by Christ; they were witnesses of the risen Jesus and caused the New Testament documents to be written and gathered together. They were an unrepeatable generation. But the work of pioneering the gospel goes on, all over the world: church planting, travelling leadership, strategy over a wide area; these continue to demand apostolic gifts. They are also necessary in the local church. If each generation is called upon to proclaim the gospel afresh, then new initiatives and apostolic gifting are vitally necessary. The person who is sent out to start the new after-school club for children, which leads to a whole new generation of families coming into contact with the church, is someone who should have an apostolic gift.

PROPHETS

Now that we are in the New Testament Age of the Spirit we do not expect prophets of the stature of Old Testament prophets like Elijah or Elisha. The revelation which they longed for is ours in the Holy Scriptures, and the presence of God which they experienced is ours as we gather for worship, and particularly in the Holy Communion. But God still speaks and his word still needs applying today. We know we are to love and serve our neighbours; we do not need a new revelation to tell us that. But how to love our neighbours, how to relate the Christian faith to local politics, to the ethical dilemmas of our particular place and time – these are all questions that need not only careful thought but also divine guidance and wisdom. When we pray together some of us will be given prophetic insights for the whole body with the result that a parish vision will become more than the sum of our individual thoughts.

EVANGELISTS

Our world is in the grip of the cynics and the bad news people. What we need are 'good news people' or evangelists. They are those who enable others to believe in the good news of God's love. Every congregation has people who could develop this gift. Most clergy do not have this gift, so unless others are encouraged to pray for it and use it, the congregation will not grow.[19]

PASTORS AND TEACHERS

Most scholars bracket these two gifts together. A pastor is a spiritual shepherd, who cares for Christ's flock by teaching them God's love. Whereas apostles, prophets and evangelists can often have travelling ministries, no church can grow without the settled and committed ministry of those who live in the local church and teach there over many years. All parochial clergy and local church ministers are called to be pastors and teachers, but only a minority of pastors and teachers need be ordained. In fact the modern Church, like the New Testament one, expects an increase in the numbers of those with pastoring and teaching gifts.

What are these ministry gifts for?

To equip the saints for the work of ministry, for building up the body of Christ, until all of us come to the unity of the faith and of the knowledge of the Son of God, to maturity, to the measure of the full stature of Christ.[20]

It is the calling of the ordained ministry and their colleagues not to do all the ministry but to enable all God's people to discover their gifts and to use them. This involves much prayer, teaching and encouragement. The more that lay people practise their gifts, and especially ministry gifts, the more that wise and authoritative leadership is needed if the result is to be unity, maturity and holiness rather than chaos and anarchy. A church that is being true to its Master will be one with apostolic gifts to pioneer, prophetic gifts to envision, evangelistic gifts to be good news to its community, pastoral gifts to care and teaching gifts to make disciples. Just as the Father is generous with his forgiveness, so the Son is a generous Head of the Church who gives spiritual gifts with great generosity to his people. The old model, where the pastor teaches alone from the pulpit, or the priest presides alone at the altar, is in danger of hiding this generous God from view. The Lord makes himself manifest as the Head of the whole body when each part is working properly.[21]

PROBLEMS WITH THE REDISCOVERY OF THE AGE OF THE SPIRIT

The fears which many ordinary Christians have about Pentecostal or charismatic renewal do have some foundation. We live in an age of the quick fix, and anything that seems to promise miracles without repentance or immediate revelation without the Scriptures is bound to be attractive for all the wrong reasons.

The fear of the liberally minded Christian that the charismatic movement is pietistic, individualistic and politically extremely right wing is not unfounded. Books on the charismatic approach to social action are thin on the ground and tend to be either superficial or dangerously wrong. Do popular churches act to change the world or do they simply reflect the culture in which they are set?

The original Pentecostal churches were churches of the poor and dispossessed; a major part of their appeal was to give power to the powerless and a family to the uprooted. Faced with the temptation to provide a spiritual version of the consumer-led therapeutic culture that encouraged North Americans and Europeans to turn in upon themselves,[22] most charismatic churches are resisting that temptation and are identifying the need to relate to a real community with an open-ended commitment of service. In some parts of England charismatic Christians have sacrificially moved into poor areas in order to empower the locals with the aid of the gospel; in many others churches have produced funds and people to do the essential social work which governments cannot afford.[23] Prison ministries, halfway houses, job-finding schemes – the charismatic churches can no longer be accused of not wanting to get their hands dirty.

The fear of the evangelical Christian that charismatics are strong on feelings but weak on teaching is understandable too. There are some churches where systematic Bible teaching has been all but abandoned. Nevertheless there is another and healthier side to this story. Many Catholic Christians have been taught through an experience of the Spirit to trust the Bible as God's word. The Bible and Christian teaching continue to form the major constituents of the programme at many of the large Christian conferences that draw so many thousands of participants.

Equally the fear of the Catholic Christian, that centuries of dignity and order in worship have been jettisoned in favour of 'happy-clappy' services, has some grounds. However, many evangelical Christians have been enabled by an experience of the Spirit to value sacraments, symbols and liturgy. The Holy Spirit has done a remarkable work of bringing together the different wings of the Western Church. It is foolish to believe, as some Christians appear to do, that because God is doing a new thing in our time he has not been powerfully present to his people in all the intervening centuries. He has. Nevertheless there are clearly high and low points in church history. Even in the New Testament period it is obvious that the living water does not flow at the same rate constantly. The words that inspired Holman Hunt to paint his most famous picture, *The Light of the World*: 'Behold, I stand at the door and knock; if any one hears my voice and opens the door, I will come in to him and eat with him, and he with me'[24] are, after all, addressed not to potential converts but to a congregation that had grown lukewarm.

TORONTO BLESSING?

In 1994 the so-called Toronto Blessing broke out at the Airport Vineyard Church in Toronto. Canadian Christians are, if anything, even less inclined than the English to be emotional in their religion. For many years this church had been praying for a revival of faith. Then something happened which drew first hundreds and then thousands of Christians to come to the nightly meetings for prayer and praise, during which people would fall to the floor or find themselves laughing or singing with a new-found sense of the presence of God.[25]

When I visited the Airport Vineyard in the summer of 1994 a profoundly deaf woman was asked to say why she kept bursting into laughter at solemn moments of the service. She explained how she had been deaf and therefore isolated all her life. When she had first come to the church, the ministry team had offered to pray for her healing, had explained what they were going to do and had laid hands on her deaf ears. The woman, however, had insisted on removing their hands from her ears and had placed them over her heart. 'First my heart,' she kept saying, 'first my heart.' When they prayed for her it was like a dam bursting inside her – and she discovered joy for the first time. That was worth a bit of disturbance in church.

It seemed to me that her prayers had been richly answered and that she now had a living and joyful relationship with her Lord. What had clearly happened was that 'religion', something external which she had heard about, had become real and internal by the power of the Holy Spirit. She had found the living water welling up inside her. Take away this power of the Holy Spirit to make the person of Jesus real in us and the word of God real to us and you are left with a dying institution and a book of unfulfilled promises.

There are, however, more similarities between traditional and charismatic spiritual experience than meet the eye. Dr Pat Dixon, who has spoken and written helpfully on the Toronto Blessing, asserts that in human beings there are three main states of consciousness: being awake, being asleep and something in between.[26] The intermediate state is commonly experienced at the point of waking or of falling asleep. Dixon says that some kinds of religious experience typically happen in that in-between state, and he cites Peter's vision on the rooftop.[27]

What happens in the Toronto Blessing and similar charismatic experiences is what Dixon calls an 'altered state of consciousness' (ASC). The long sessions of praise and prayer encourage an altered state of consciousness. Then when the Spirit is invoked and helpers gather round the worshipper for several minutes praying for blessing it is not perhaps surprising that the worshipper is particularly receptive to manifestations of the Spirit. Those who are not used to charismatic worship often react against it strongly because of the potential for self-deception or external manipulation when emotions are released. Although these dangers are obvious and real, they are not as great as the danger that the sceptical church will miss an important route that an incarnational God uses to reveal himself to flesh and blood.

In ordinary churches too the careful listener will find that altered states of consciousness are not uncommon. Why does that woman always sit in the same pew, where she cannot hear or see very well? Because she has always sat there and, during the Creed when we say the words 'the communion of saints', she can feel the presence of her long-dead father and mother who used to sit beside her. Why does this man protest when the band leaves a music-stand directly in front of his seat? Because when the sun shines through a particular pane of stained glass during morning service, time suddenly stands still and he knows that God is real. Why does the caretaker enjoy spending time polishing a particular table in the sanctuary? Because as he does so his present troubles seem to melt away and he is confronted by the love of God. The liturgy, the music, the sacraments, the buildings of traditional worship are great encouragers of low-level ASCs. We clergy are guilty of monumental self-deception, far greater than the potential self-deception of charismatics, if we think that most people come to church only or mainly for the reasons that we think should draw them. The experience of such low-level ASCs is of course why people often protest beyond all apparent reason when clergy want to change things. We are not aware (and they do not want to tell us) that the reason they cannot cope with our proposal to move the font or change the Lord's Prayer is because that particular arrangement of things is for them the trigger to an experience just as important as 'being slain in the Spirit' for the charismatic. The task of the church leader is not to suppress such experiences but to help interpret them within a framework of orthodox doctrine.

It is a commonplace of art history that artists have purported to depict saints at ecstasy in prayer when in fact they were 'really' painting people (usually women) in sexual ecstasy. Bernini's statue of *The Ecstasy of St Teresa*, recording the vision from her auto-biography, and Poussin's painting of *The Annunciation* are oft-cited examples.[28] I thought of this when we began to be accustomed to the sight of people lying out on the floor, waiting upon God in tranquil ecstasy – and the memory of Bernini's masterpiece returned to me. These people on the floor of their parish church were obviously not faking anything – most of them had never heard of Bernini – but there was that same kind of expression on their faces. Could it be that the relationship is in fact the other way round? We post-Freudians assume that spiritual experience is only a pale reflection of the 'real' delights of physical orgasm. But could it perhaps also be, as saints of previous ages have dared to maintain, that the greatest ecstasies of sexual intercourse are but a shadow and foretaste of the delights of mystical union with God – the great lover? Previous generations of saints had long been aware of this in their readings of the Song of Songs – but somehow we had missed it.[29]

TESTING FOR THE GENUINE

The question that was repeatedly put to me while the so-called Toronto Blessing was at its height was, How do we judge it? It seems to me now as it did then that the tests needed for this extra-ordinary phenomenon could well be applied to the charismatic movement in general and in fact should be precisely the same as those enjoined on us by the New Testament for the testing of anything that purports to be from God.

a) *What are the fruits?* Most of the church leaders in my parish discovered a more lively relationship with God than before as a result of the Toronto experience; for many of them it was also more profound and touched areas of life that had hitherto been untouched. Very many ordinary churchgoers discovered new spiritual gifts. Perhaps a larger number still began to think of their church more as a movement and less as a club.

b) *What is the teaching, and is it in agreement with the teaching of the Church down the ages based on the Bible?* It was, I believe, a rediscovery of neglected parts of the Scriptures. Obviously the dramatic side effects led some to put undue emphasis on these parts, but generally the phenomena were handled with dignity and humour in most ordinary British churches touched by the revival.

c) *What effect has this on a church?* Here is my list: First, a greater desire to receive from God and to wait upon him. Second, a greater desire to worship him. Third, a greater expectancy that he can transform our lives. Fourth, a greater desire to listen attentively to his word. Fifth, a greater desire to meet for prayer with other Christians. Yes, there were some problems and some not so good results, but nothing as bad as in Corinth, and the good outweighed the bad.

One of the keys to judging both the transient effects of the Toronto Blessing and the more long-lasting effects of the charismatic movement is to apply Paul's wise instruction to 'test everything about it; keeping what is good, and sifting out what is bad'.[30] We are quite accustomed to sifting a sermon, taking the good and discarding the bad. Just because the preacher begins, 'In the Name of the Father, and of the Son and of the Holy Spirit', it does not mean she is not human or that her words are infallible. They have to be tested. This is all the more important with spiritual gifts.

Any local church that encourages them will need systems in place so that they can be practised in safe environments where all-too-human prophecies and interpretations can be weighed and measured, and where the faithful can be protected against well-meaning but harmful 'words' from self-styled prophets. As the new churches have discovered, the greater the liberty the more we need discipline.

In the sweep of church history, the great revivals have lasted only a comparatively short time. They are fragile phenomena. It was hard to keep up the pace or the intensity. But undoubtedly their effects have been long-lasting. And it is clearer now than it was how much the Toronto Blessing was prepared for in prayer over many years. I remember a black bishop at my theological college who had been caught up in the first stages of the East African Revival. I asked him what had happened after it had died down. 'During the revival we used to run from village to village with the good news of the Saviour,' he said. 'These days we walk. But it is still the same gospel!'

In the twenty-first century, fewer people are willing to commit themselves to a church, but more are open about their (sometimes strange) spiritual experiences. Today Christian leaders are required who can help people to interpret and sift their experiences by referring them to Christ. In any parish, time spent with people, listening to their stories, will reveal many things happening below the surface. Relating their stories to the Bible and the fulfilment of the Old Testament prophecies in Christ can enable them to start to hear his voice in their lives more clearly and to put them on the path of discipleship. Christians long for wise leaders who can help them in their relationship with God, who will enable them to discover their gifts, practise them in the safe environment of the church and use them to share God's love in the world.

3

Leading Uncommon Worship

A SUNDAY IN THE LIFE

Not a good start. The door bell went at 12.30 a.m. – a young man wanting to sleep in our basement. We keep a sleeping bag and a foam mattress for all comers, but it took a little while to settle him for the night.

Sunday normally starts more slowly than other days; time for a leisurely shower before arriving in church at 7.30 a.m. The sacristan has already opened up and is quietly laying the holy table; it is part of her worship, preparing for the great messianic feast. Shortly afterwards the deputy warden and sidesmen appear. There was a time when the 8 a.m. congregation was decreasing and I had to prepare everything myself, so I explained to them that we would have to close unless they helped. They rose to the challenge and now this quiet service with a congregation of anything between 10 and 25 is an oasis of prayer and stillness before the noise and bustle of the other services. It is also the time when I am most aware of the communion of saints.

At present we alternate between the Book of Common Prayer and the new liturgy, without hymns or music. But we do have a short homily and, being generally an unspontaneous speaker, I use this service as a kind of spiritual exercise to speak extempore, reading through the lessons before the start and delivering a two-minute address with a single point. Often it works, and when it doesn't I console myself that half the congregation is going deaf and the other half deliberately sits too far away to hear me anyway.

Cynics say that eight o'clockers hate humanity, because the few present spread themselves round the church so that they can be as private as possible. But that is not true; it is simply that they are more reserved and prefer a more austere form of service. I know this because a few years ago a curate unwittingly started a minor revolution by inviting the eight o'clockers to pass the Peace. She did not know the battles that had been fought at the other services and how the early communion was a refuge for those who hate demonstrative worship. I waited for the explosion. Into my mind came a new Bateman cartoon: 'The curate who invited the eight o'clock congregation to exchange the Peace'. But to my amazement they took to embracing and kissing one another as if it were the most natural thing in the world. For many of them it is their only physical contact in the whole week with another human being.

Today there are 22 communicants, mainly in their seventies and eighties, and I know them all, faithful servants of God, who have seen the world and the church change round them and have remained loyal to their Lord. It is a privilege, as Newman said, to share with them the Bread of Life. At the end I greet everyone; one woman is worried about a hospital appointment so we go to the lady chapel for a special prayer.

There is time for a quick bowl of cereal and a mug of tea with Jane before dashing down to the school hall at the other end of the parish where we have a 9.30 a.m. family service. The team has already put out the chairs; the holy table (a trestle table during the week) and lectern (a music-stand) are decked out in their beautiful frontal and fall, and the candle is ready to be lit. With a minimum of ecclesiastical furniture a scruffy school hall can seem right for worship. The coffee is steaming in the corner, the overhead projector is being unfolded and the children's music group is practising. The service leaders pray together in the staff room before emerging at 9.30 a.m., for all the world like Baptist deacons, except that there is not a suit in sight. People keep on arriving and we are full by 9.40 a.m., a cheerful crowd of young and old, with plenty of noisy children until they leave for their own instruction. The new curate has a way of making everyone feel at ease, and the other members of the team lead their parts with dignity. I enjoy preaching here, because they are so appreciative; when 35 adults are almost near enough for me to touch them, the rapport is immediate.

At 10.30 a.m. it is time to pick up a couple of junior choir members and drive back to the parish church. As we negotiate the Sunday morning streets I think of all the country parsons who have miles of lanes to cover. When we arrive the preparations for an infant baptism are in full swing – except that somehow we have mislaid the form with the name of the baby! Welcoming 250 people is a demanding business and already the church is buzzing with stewards, musicians, people testing microphones, youth leaders fetching materials, and early arrivals, some of them from long-stay homes. I reflect that life is much more exciting than it used to be now that we have so much congregational participation, but it is also more stressful as people forget to turn up or arrive late for their duties. But the young couple have made real steps of faith and have brought all their family to hear them make their promises. All of us have doubts about infant baptism from time to time but today you can see it at its best. The 9.30 a.m. sermon is repeated and I can see that everyone is touched by the issue; several come up for prayer later.

Afterwards there are crowds of people to meet as usual and it is nearly 1 p.m. before we close up. At lunch we have a girl who is applying to be a pastoral assistant with the youth for a year. If she can cope with vicarage lunch she should be able to cope with most social occasions. In the middle of the afternoon I put her on the London train and then there is a couple of hours to relax before the prayer ministry team arrives at 5.30 p.m. to prepare for the evening service.

At present we have a plainly provisional evening pattern of worship with three separate but connected congregations. The adult congregation of 70 to 100 meets in the church building. The service falls into three parts of 20 minutes each: first comes the evening office, then the band leads enthusiastic singing, finally there is a sermon. Or, almost finally. A significant proportion stay behind to pray with others and then to have coffee with one another. The second congregation is the 18–25s group who also number up to 100; we can hear their singing because it is louder than ours. The third (in the church hall) is the younger teenage group, which has expanded enormously; their parents are an important part of the adult congregation. When all three congregations meet together the church is full and we have a tremendous sense of the variety of God's people!

Jane co-ordinates the teams who lead the prayer ministry after the service but on most Sundays we manage to be back home by

9 p.m. for an important family tradition: sandwiches all together in front of the television. A detective story with plenty of excitement helps us relax. We have had contact with over 500 people today – but ultimately it is not our responsibility.

WRONG NOTES

All your works shall give thanks to you, O LORD,
and all your faithful shall bless you.[1]

Worship tests the leaders of a local church like nothing else. I have never known a church without tensions over worship. There are disputes over order versus spontaneity, over language old and new and, sharpest of all, over music. In all these arguments the purpose of worship can quickly fade into the background as factions jostle for their preferences. Clergy and lay leaders find themselves having to hold the peace between different pressure groups and then being accused of indecision. I remember well the despondent look on the face of one of my training vicars as he opened the letters of complaint about the Sunday services in his study on a Monday morning. For onlookers it is deeply disturbing that the praise of the one God should so divide Christians; but perhaps it is not so surprising that the Enemy should particularly delight to have it so.

The beginning of a solution is to step back and to teach what worship is. In fact worship and teaching, like word and sacrament, go together.[2] One of the consequences of our fallen nature is that we cannot consistently worship unselfconsciously any more than we can give ourselves wholeheartedly to any act or relationship:

> Lips that would kiss
> Form prayers to broken stone . . .
> Between the motion
> And the act
> Falls the Shadow.[3]

We have to be given a fresh vision of what worship is and then be frequently reminded of it.

WORSHIP IS ...

One of the most universal of human experiences is to stand looking up at the skies on a starry night, to be conscious of being only a very small part of something infinitely wonderful and to attempt to reach out to the One who made, sustains and cares for all this.[4] Worship is the response of the creature to the Creator; to worship is to desire to give true worth to what is beyond our powers of appreciation. To worship is to be aware of the heavens declaring the glory of God. To worship is to be aware of the transcendence of God: the infinite distance between the maker and the made; and at the same time his immanence: to be part of a creation that longs to respond properly to God at work in it. Indeed there is nothing more attractive, even compelling, to outsiders than real worship in spirit and in truth. In that sense a worshipping church is evangelistic long before it sets up an outreach committee.

Christian worship adds to this natural wonder and awe a sense of gratitude to God for restoring through Christ the relationship that we have spoiled.[5] We have the indescribable privilege of joining Jesus in saying 'Abba' to his Father and ours; this is worship in the Spirit.

The Lambeth bishops were surely wrong when in 1998 they announced that evangelism was the first task of the Church. Worship is the first priority and highest calling of the Church. It is the first and great commandment. Evangelism is about helping people to turn from worship of self or of idols to the worship of the living God. Praise of the God and Father of our Lord Jesus Christ is, in the phrase of C. S. Lewis, 'inner health made audible'.[6]

In US films there is the moment at a wedding when the minister turns to the groom and says, 'You may now kiss the bride.' At that moment, with different degrees of awkwardness and enthusiasm, the bride and groom express the relationship between them and their commitment for the future. In a similar way our services highlight, embody and renew that relationship between us and God which is worked out in the whole of our lives. Our lives are made to be a response to the One who lovingly made us and yet more lovingly redeemed us. On Sundays we reorient our lives, reset our compasses, so that the week can increasingly be lived out as an act of worship: as the response in our lives to the love that we have received through Christ. It is the calling of those who lead in worship to serve in such a way that the people see themselves as the bride, coming to kiss and to be kissed by the groom.

Humanity has a special role in the created order. If we humans do not recognize Jesus going to the cross as the Son of God, then the very stones will cry out.[7] Psalm 8 speaks of us as being the deputy-leaders of creation and of God as putting everything under our feet. The letter to the Hebrews takes up this theme, reminding us that we have not lived up to our vocation and that therefore 'we do not yet see everything in subjection to him'. But 'we see Jesus', as Saviour and Model of what we may become.[8] In the Age of the Spirit, the creation 'waits with eager longing for the revealing of the children of God', waits for our lives to be in tune with our calling. Equally the Spirit helps us as we express our frustration at constantly falling short of our vocation and aids us in the weakness of our worship.[9] In turning our lives into acts of worship, we are becoming the conscious representatives of Christ, fulfilling our destiny as stewards of creation and anticipating that day when Christ will be all in all, when creation will be fully back in tune with the God of love who made it.

The rabbis tell stories about peasants caught in a life of grinding poverty and debt who discover that in the future they will inherit great wealth. In the interim the lawyers arrange for them to live like princes for one day a week. For six days life goes on as before – hard labour and heavy burdens – but on the seventh they celebrate their real and future identity. So on the Christian Sabbath we receive our resurrection life and celebrate our identity as children of God.

Although worship is deeply personal it is also corporate. Here too those 'who have the first fruits of the Spirit'[10] have a representative function in the wider society. Worship is not to be relegated to the private sphere. One of the delusions of our culture is that we are both a pluralist society in which many different religions can coexist and a secular society in which no religion may intrude on to the public stage. But we cannot live in a value-free society; the problem about pretending we do is that unexamined values and religious assumptions have to be smuggled in somewhere.

Our society is no less religious than any other; it is just that the idols we bow down to are largely unrecognized – and therefore more subtly dangerous. Politicians like to pay lip service to the need for community values, but in practice regularly give greatest heed to Mammon in its latest reincarnation, popularly known as the global market: a juggernaut that crushes regions and small nations and destroys communities in ever more aggressive appeals to individual selfishness. Football used to be a matter of teams representing various cities competing against each other. Now it is a matter of the richest companies buying up the best players and crushing those who cannot afford to compete. We have created an idol in the field of sport, which demands more and more from us for less and less return. Public worship reminds us that there are more important values in sport than money.

Another example of the importance of public worship is the vexed question of school assemblies. Many teachers assume that Christian worship is out of place in a secular society. It is inappropriate, they say, to force children to worship. But problems with assembly are only a symptom of the loss of agreement about the purpose of education in general and the curriculum in particular. What are the competing value systems behind decisions to change curricula or methods of testing pupils? Why is it that some parts of the school programme are optional and others compulsory? The public and objective worship of God each day enables a school community to reach beyond either the politics of the county or the theories of the current head teacher. It allows every child (and teacher) to know he or she is loved, has a variety of abilities and gifts and immense potential.

Christians who meet to worship in their local churches are a peaceful but powerful counter-demonstration. We show that there are greater values than those, for instance, of the marketplace or the survival of the fittest. As the spires of village churches point heavenwards, so our services give worth-ship to One who judges us by different standards. The Eucharist, during which the unemployed labourer and the captain of industry kneel side by side to eat from the same loaf, is a political act. The body of Christ reunites the community, which our body politic often fractures.

Because Christianity has been part of the warp and weft of our schooling, our political establishment and our landscape for so long, it is easy to miss the challenge that worship presents to our culture. If Jesus is Lord of all, then we are declaring him Lord of the marketplace as well as of our private lives, Lord of here and now as well as of the world to come. In other parts of the globe this is much clearer. I remember a diocesan trip to Vladimir in the old Soviet Union, where it seemed to us visitors as if the only colour and life in the lives of Russians caught up in an endless sea of decaying, grey concrete were provided by the Orthodox Church. Our translator told us how, in order to have a Christian wedding without losing her university post, she had to be married 200 miles from home in a different state. Worship not only opens a door into the eternal; it also brings the kingdom of God uncomfortably close to the rival kingdoms and false gods of our lives.

We live in a time when community life is failing and the barren anonymity of city life is increasingly characteristic of life in the suburbs and country too. With such a social context it is not surprising that calling people together to worship is both difficult and immensely worthwhile. Humans can only truly be community when they share values and worth; it is in the Pentecostal worship of Christ that divided humanity can be reunited in the Spirit. All this needs teaching carefully and regularly if congregations are not to treat services as products for consumers.

WORDS AND MUSIC

In our house we have radios in different rooms. When our children come into the kitchen they will switch off the news or the classical music and turn to commercial music stations. If the whole family is gathered in one room then hard choices have to be made! So it is with the different cultures of worship. Hard choices have to be made, about set liturgies versus spontaneity, about traditional and contemporary language, and about music styles.

LITURGY AND SPONTANEITY

Why do most churches in the world have set liturgies – words that are fixed? Surely worship should be from the heart? In all my churches there have been people who have never understood the point of a liturgy and who have longed for 'the freedom of the Spirit'. Those who go to conferences and hear speakers from the new churches often return feeling that liturgical worship is not only boring but wrong:

> We are not under a covenant of law with rules and regulations laid down, but under a covenant of grace that operates by the direct leading of the Holy Spirit. Now some would argue that the liturgies that the Church has developed over generations are the result of the Spirit's leading. But such liturgies are by their nature legalistic; some are even upheld by ecclesiastical law. The Holy Spirit never leads us into legalism. Satan is the arch-legalist. He takes advantage of our human tendency to slip back into the flesh and would bewitch us into replacing a Spirit led and Spirit inspired worship with a rigid frame, ritualistic ceremonies and dead observances.[11]

In the last 20 years the leaders of many new churches have become more appreciative of the strengths of a set liturgy, but the question still stands. Why do we address God with formal speeches or 'second-hand' words, rather than with the intimacy and spontaneity of 'Abba, Father'? The answer is in the Bible itself. Worship is patterning myself on Christ. Being a disciple is making God's word live in my life, learning to declare the mighty acts of God for myself. When God brought his people out of Egypt he gave them a set of actions and set words to say. 'When your children ask you, "What do you mean by this observance?" you shall say, "It is the passover sacrifice to the LORD."'[12] Psalm 119 tells us to meditate on the law of the Lord day and night and 'incline our hearts to keep this law' (Book of Common Prayer). Is such repetition vain or insincere? Of course not.

So too the New Testament worship is full of Old Testament words and phrases; there is continuity, as we would expect. The early Christians devoted themselves to the Jewish liturgical prayers,[13] and our own prayers have grown up from this root. When the early Christians had a Spirit-filled prayer meeting they praised God in the words of a set psalm,[14] and we have continued to do so ever since. Even in heaven we will find, according to Revelation, that the worship there is liturgical.[15] Liturgical worship reminds us that we are neither the first generation nor the last to worship the Almighty. The rhythms of the seasons are marked by the rhythms of the Church's year in a way that gives a rich and balanced diet of worship.

Paradoxically, to have set words sets us free to worship in the Spirit. I am of that generation that still knows a great deal of the 1662 Prayer Book by heart, and I find that, because I know the words, and know that they are good and true, I am set free to worship. Liturgy permits the congregation to participate actively; as the US bishop said, 'The people get to shout back at the preacher!' They find the set words do not tie them down but release the poet in them. When St Paul says, 'Where the Spirit of the Lord is, there is liberty',[16] he is not saying that proper worship is freedom from set prayers. He is saying that there is the freedom to have a real relationship with the Lord, to enter the holy of holies, and to join in the song of the angels: 'Glory to God in the highest'.

But of course it is not either one or the other; it is a failure of the local church if Christians are not trained to pray in their own words as well as being equipped to use the treasury of resources from the past. A balanced diet will include opportunities for spontaneous contributions, offerings of gifts of the Spirit, and times of more intimate prayer and silence as well as set liturgies. Certainly cell groups and small congregations make it easier for individual contributions than larger, more formal groupings. The *Common Worship* services of the Church of England recognize this need for balance and allow great flexibility, including provision for testimony, open prayer and gifts of the Spirit when appropriate.

Freedom and order in worship are not opposites but allies. When people know where they are they have a firm platform from which to go out and explore. From many visits to the new churches I have seen that the ones that work are those where the leaders are strong and directive and where the congregation have confidence that the worship leader can handle interruption. Although there is no printed liturgy there is certainly a pattern, which the regulars know and expect. As with liturgical services it can also grow stale.

WORDS OLD AND NEW

Among the majority of Christians for whom liturgical worship is important there is a split between those who are attached to the old words and those who prefer the new. For traditional Roman Catholics the Latin Mass retains a dignity and majesty that make the new English rites seem banal by comparison. For many Anglicans the language of the sixteenth-century Book of Common Prayer still has a power and a beauty that enable them to worship the majesty and holiness of God in a way that no modern language service can achieve.

It is true that much contemporary English is prosaic and humdrum. Journalists and scholars enjoy poking fun at the clumsiness and bathos of modern renderings of the Bible and the liturgy.[17] The Prayer Book and the Authorized Version of the Bible are still hugely popular but there are important reasons why most of us cannot simply go back to using them for our main services. The first is that most people no longer understand them. It is not the fault of the Church that the universal teaching of Chaucer and Shakespeare was largely stopped in schools in the 1970s and 1980s. We have to deal with the results, and teach that 'common worship' should be in the language of the people. Those who have been brought up in public schools with daily chapel think they still understand the old language. But I often go to services where lay people insist on reading lessons from the Authorized Version and the way in which they read betrays that they do not understand.

The supporters of the use of the old language Bible and Prayer Book often point out that the Church was stronger and more respected in previous centuries and argue that to go back to the tradition will help revive the faith in our time. I believe the truth to be rather the opposite. It is the experience of God that moves poets and painters to create great works of art. It was the fire of conviction that produced the wonderful language, not the other way around. If we abandon the traditions and fail to teach them to our children then we disinherit future generations. But if we do not allow the present generation to express their own experience of God in their own language then we imprison them in the past.

I have never forgotten the boredom I felt as a child whenever we went to church and had to go through the long pages of the Prayer Book services. We who have grown to love the familiar words and have made them part of our relationship with the Lord are naturally unwilling to face what a barrier the things we love can be to new and young Christians.

I have to confess my own deep prejudice on two counts. First, I shudder at the ungrammatical when it comes to addressing the Almighty (and have to keep reminding myself that much of the New Testament was written in rough *koine* Greek). Second, I find very trying those hymnologists who tamper with the texts of old hymns in an attempt to bring them up to date. They seem to have little ear for poetry or rhythm and their results are often insensitive in the extreme. My least favourite example is:

> Rock of Ages, split in two,
> Let me hide myself in you.

I am glad to say that I have not yet seen this one in print – but others come close to it in reducing the sublime to the banal.

STYLES OF MUSIC

Singing and music are essential in worship. It is so weak to say 'Alleluia' rather than sing it! True Christian music will challenge the standards of the culture: the easy commercialism of much so-called Christian music on the one hand, or the raising of certain forms of music almost to the status of a religion on the other. Both need to be challenged.[18]

The English choral tradition, exemplified by the annual televised Christmas Carol Service at King's College, Cambridge, has been so successful that it is difficult for many people to imagine Anglican worship without it. Of course in parish churches these days the choir will have few small boys, and the parishioners do not queue for hours to be sure of a seat. Nevertheless it is the robed choir, occupying the chancel and leading Victorian hymns in four parts, which is somehow fixed in many people's minds as how worship should be.

It is important therefore to recognize that the Service of Lessons and Carols at King's, Cambridge, is a twentieth-century invention and that most of our 'traditional' hymns and music are less than 200 years old. The hymn as we know it is largely a result of the Evangelical Revival of the eighteenth century. The church choir is mainly a result of the Gothic Revival of the nineteenth.

There are real disadvantages for local churches in the modern English choral tradition. One is that four-part settings are too high for men to be able to sing the tune. The effect of this difficulty should not be underestimated: it is an unspoken way of saying that men are not welcome in our pews. And if men cannot sing the tune, then almost no one beyond the choir can sing the psalms. In many places evening worship has died because no one knew what to do about replacing a form that effectively prevented the people from singing the psalter. One of the urgent tasks for the Church, locally and nationally, is to find new and varied ways of singing the Scriptures again, and especially the psalms. I do not myself think it beyond the wit of an enthusiastic congregation to learn tunes to the canticles and to the main songs in the Holy Communion plus half a dozen of the best Anglican chants – but many in my congregations disagree with me!

There are whole sections of society and entire age groups who simply do not relate to English choral music. As the report *Faith in the City* put it, the style of our worship is an almost impenetrable barrier for most urban people.[19] Cathedrals and cathedral music are one of the success stories of our time. Countless people have been led to worship God through them; it would be a tragedy if the nation stopped supporting the choir schools and the broadcast of cathedral services. They are called to be centres of excellence and innovation for their dioceses. But they cannot be the only model for most local churches, if only because congregations are not permitted to sing the service along with a cathedral choir.

At their best, church choirs help enormously in the leading of services. They channel enthusiasm for worship; they enable people who do not want to sit passively in a pew to contribute something active in the church, and they use people's gifts for singing. At their worst they can be centres of disharmony in a church, resistant to the very kind of change that brought them into being 150 years ago. In some places they are as out of date as the wireless or the radiogram.

But the important question to ask in a local church is not 'How can we maintain our musical tradition?' but rather 'How can we best enable the people in this place to sing the praises of God?' The answer will vary from place to place. Where there is still a strong choral tradition the choir will be an important part of the answer. In most places, however, there will probably need to be several groups of singers and instrumentalists, with a variety of menus for different services and age groups, reflecting the variety of gifts of the Spirit that are being poured out among us. I have known children's bands, jazz bands, orchestral groups, chorale groups and gospel groups in churches, according to local talent and vision. It would be a mistake to exclude any of these from the range of possibilities. A well-played violin or a horn, a good solo voice or duet, can transform worship.

I remember one organist who dismissed modern electronic music, not only on the usual grounds of lowering the standards and offering second-rate to Almighty God, but also because the new songs were 'inspired by rock music, which is of the Devil'. This is worth a closer look. It is true that groups who attempt to sing Christian words to a style of music born of violent protest and hard drugs are unlikely to commend themselves to churches (though even these are a relief after some of the sugary muzak that wallpapers Christian bookshops and exhibitions). But one of the insufficiently known stories of the Christian faith is how the slaves on the North American plantations transformed the 'lining out' of the psalms into negro spirituals, and how these spirituals developed – with the help of the *klezmer* music of another group of oppressed people, Jewish refugees from Eastern Europe – into jazz, then soul, pop and rock. The music of the chain gangs and the cotton fields was essentially responsorial, like the psalms. In the Puritan tradition, brought over from Britain, the cantor would sing a line of a psalm and the congregation would sing it back. The slaves adapted this and, out of the curious and painful paradox of a gospel of salvation plus slavery, was born the spiritual.[20] 'Go down, Moses', 'Swing low, sweet chariot', 'Steal away' and all the rest were about the justice and freedom of God's kingdom breaking into a world of pain and rebellion. In the end, the music won. Slave music conquered the world.

This of course takes us back to the beginnings of salvation history. Bible worship comes from the Hebrew slave people in Egypt and Babylon. It comes from the little, oppressed Christian sect who overturned the mighty Roman Empire. The call-and-response of Redeemer and redeemed is still the heartbeat of worship today.

One of the missed opportunities of *Common Worship* is that so little of it is properly responsorial. Anglican rites from other parts of the world, particularly Africa, have risen to this challenge more successfully. Another challenge, left over from the Reformation divide, is to enable congregations to sing the liturgy. On the whole in the Western Church, Protestant churches punctuate the liturgy with hymns, while Catholics sing parts of the liturgy. St Augustine was right when he said that to sing is to pray twice: to set parts of the liturgy to music unifies the whole act of worship, enables the worshipper to appropriate the words and sets the spirit free.

So there is a teaching and a learning to be done if congregations today are to appreciate the work of the Spirit in our musical traditions. The little quarrels of the comfortable church are perhaps themselves a symptom of a deeper spiritual problem. Somehow the distilling needed to produce great art rarely comes from comfort and complacency! Just as the negro spiritual came from slavery, so it may be the poor and oppressed in our own society who will produce the next wave of Spirit-filled music in worship.

But the principles remain the same. If worship is to express the heart of the response of the community to God then there will be two poles. One is what God has revealed to us by the Spirit in creation, in Scripture and supremely in Christ. The other is the heart-cry of his people. The question we are to ask as we prepare music for worship is not 'What music do we like?' but rather 'What music would enable the community we are set among to express its worship of God if it started coming to worship?' That question produces a very different kind of answer!

The sign of the coming kingdom is 'when the true worshippers will worship the Father in spirit and truth, for such the Father seeks to worship him'.[21] Far more important to God than order versus spontaneity, language old or new, music ancient or modern, is the heart of the worshippers. The creation of a worshipping community in the desert of isolated lives is a true delight both to the worshippers and to their Redeemer.

LEADING WORSHIP

Leading the worship of God's people is both a great privilege and a daunting burden. There is a telling ambiguity about the word 'focus' as it is sometimes used in documents about the doctrine of ministry. When those who lead us in worship do it right, then they are transparent like a lens, enabling us the worshippers to 'focus' more closely on the Lord. When they do it wrong, then they become the 'focus of attention', like a spoiled child at a party.

To lead worship we must first be worshippers ourselves. Before Moses could be used as God's mouthpiece to Pharaoh and to his people, he was taken into the desert and saw the burning bush at Horeb. He could not have led his people to that mountain if he had not been there himself. So too we cannot invite our friends on to holy ground unless we have trodden there ourselves. Before David became king he was a singer and musician. When the ark of God was brought up to Jerusalem, King David forgot his dignity and leapt and danced and shouted before the Lord.[22] He was a man after God's heart because he did not lose the habit of worshipping God in spirit and in truth.

The thing I am most grateful for to the first vicar I worked with as a curate (Mac Farmborough) was the way in which he led worship. You could tell that he himself had come fresh from the presence of God and was now going to lead us into that presence. It helped that he had a strong sense of the invisible angels. Sometimes we laughed at him for this – Anglicans do not major on angels – but in our Sunday worship when Mac led it was diffi-cult not to be aware that the church was full of the presence of the heavenly host, and that we were privileged to be able to join our songs to the great song at the throne of God. It sounds obvious but I learned afresh that to lead worship you have to be a worshipper.

To lead worship is to serve God's people. The word 'minister' has connotations of the word 'waiter', which we have largely lost. If the task of a priest is to present God to the people and the people to God, then the task of a Christian minister is to wait on God and

to wait on his people. In a restaurant a good waiter enables the
diners and the chef to commune through the medium of the meal.
So, too, leading worship properly allows true communion between
worshippers and their Lord.

I was an altar server at St Paul's, Addlestone, in my early teens
and my vicar, John Atkins, deeply impressed me. He was full of
down-to-earth humour but before the service, while he vested in
the tiny sacristy by the door and the people made their way into
church, there was a solemn silence as he prayed his way into his
robes, and we children felt the weight of his vocation. A few
moments later as we knelt beside him at the altar and prepared for
the service we would say Psalm 43 together. At the time it seemed
strange that he said, 'Give sentence with me, O God, and defend
my cause against the ungodly people.' It was only later that I
understood the burden that serving those people laid upon him,
and how he had to wrestle with depression as well as with joy in
enabling them to worship.

The delight of the good worship leader is not to have one's own
choice of liturgy or music but to have what is best for the community. That will not be the choice of the powerful or the lowest
common denominator, but will stretch and challenge all. Just as a
mother will sacrifice her own tastes when she cooks the family meal
so the parish priest will seek out what is going to be most nourishing. Unlike a mother with young children, though, there will be
consultation and working together with the church council to
develop the right menus.

If we are attentive to God and to his people it will soon become
evident that to lead worship effectively is to discover and enable
gifts of leadership in others. While the incumbent and PCC (in
an Anglican setting) have the duty to oversee the worship and
to check that what is done is done with proper authority, *Common
Worship* allows great freedom for more and more people to share
leadership. If Anglicans on a Sunday morning are not quite in the
position of the house church at Corinth where Paul noted that
everyone in the church family had a public contribution to make,[23]
we are certainly a long way from the traditional situation where
the priest spoke and the people listened and said, 'Amen'.

WORSHIP AND REACHING OUT

I went for the first time to a church in a scruffy area of Bristol. It was an evening service and there were perhaps 35 people in a church that had been built for hundreds. After about ten minutes I recognized that there was something strange about the way in which the vicar, who had only recently come to the parish, was conducting the service. It took me the next ten minutes to work out what it was: he was leading an act of worship as if the building were full of people. Not that he ignored the congregation there. He simply communicated by the way he spoke that God had given him a vision that this church was being called to be of significance for the whole of that community in Bristol. As I pondered that service during the next week, I understood two things which have never left me. First, that to lead worship you need a vision of where the church is called to go. And second, that a church leader is responsible for leading worship in a way that caters not just for the people who are there but also for the people who are not yet there.[24] To lead worship is always to lead attention towards God's concern beyond the church to the world.

A few weeks later I was in another Bristol city church for evening service. We were greeted at the door by a steward who remarked that we were among friends and that there were 'no unsaved people in this congregation'. I was not quick enough to reply, 'Then the church can't be doing its job!' But I felt it. To worship a God who made the whole universe and conceived of the cross must involve an outflow of love, service and welcome to the community around. It was no surprise to hear a few years later that the first church I visited had indeed become full, and that the second had closed.

It is often said that people in the West do not go to church any more. It is much more accurate to say that they do not stay. It is surprising how many visitors come through a church in the course of a year, trying us out, seeking something. Recent surveys from the north of England show that as many as 40 per cent of people present in some Anglican churches are not regular worshippers. If these visitors do not sense that there is more going on than a leisure-time activity by a group of people who have their own arcane language and musical idiom then it is no wonder that they do not often give us a second try.

USING SPIRITUAL GIFTS IN WORSHIP

What then, brethren? When you come together, each one has a hymn, a lesson, a revelation, a tongue, or an interpretation. Let all things be done for edification.[25]

Worship is not something that comes from hiring the best singers and musicians. It is something that comes from the heart, from the relationship of God to us and of us to our neighbours. Where the leaders are properly serving the people, they will be enabled to contribute: to bring their offering of praise and worship, and to be able to develop their spiritual gifts so that they in turn can serve God and serve his people.

Numbers have something to do with this. St Paul probably had an extended household in mind as the base unit for a church, with perhaps between ten and 30 members. The modern equivalent would be a housegroup or cell church. Here it would be considered an unhealthy gathering if there were not an opportunity for all to contribute in an active way to the life of the group. When a congregation grows above 40, however, it can be difficult for more than a few to bring spontaneous contributions without disruption.

It can start very simply. In many churches the children come in after a time apart and are encouraged to show the adults what they have learned. In a similar way a congregation can become used to adults being asked to give an account of what God is doing in their lives. For instance, instead of the Creed in Advent or Lent, there was a custom in one church I belonged to of asking a series of Christians to give a brief account of why they were believers, or how they related their faith to their work. Then it was not too great a step for people to ask for prayer when tragedy struck, and to give thanks when there were answers to prayer. Of course leaders have to be prepared to shorten or omit other elements in a service if 'unprogrammed' contributions are made.

The more enthusiastic the worship and praise become, with

accompanying rise in volume, the more important periods of silence become too. In these precious moments of silence, when a whole congregation reflects on a reading, or simply waits upon God, it should not surprise us too much if he speaks to members of the church. In a house meeting or small church these things come naturally – a word, a tongue, a picture – they can be contributed and evaluated. In a larger church these too will need sensitive handling.

FUTURE DIRECTIONS

If worship is first and foremost to do with our response to God, then it will be something that is ever-changing and developing. We are work in progress. Communities, too, have to develop or die. The process by which they move on together under the influence of the Spirit is probably more important than the particular choices about worship that they make. Developing an atmosphere of mutual confidence in which musicians, singers, worship leaders and congregations can offer worship is a key task of church leaders. When, for instance, the pipe organ in our parish church finally collapses and will need £75,000 spent on it, the decision whether or not to raise that sum will depend on the quality of those relationships. If the organist and the choir begin by saying that the money could perhaps be better spent in Africa, and if the members of the band begin by saying how much the worship of the church would be impoverished by the loss of the organ, then the Spirit will truly be present!

There is no reason at all why the shape and order of liturgical services cannot provide space and opportunity for the Holy Spirit to speak and act, for silence and music, liturgy and spontaneity. The Anglican *Common Worship* services offer precisely this opportunity. They provide a clear shape and much good material, but leave the responsibility for the content to the local church. The only problem is that they present such a richness and variety of material that many churches will be tempted to fill all the time with written liturgy and leave too little time for silence and for the spontaneous, for the gifts of the Spirit and open prayer.

At present the tendency among some Anglican charismatic churches is to abandon liturgy and hymns and to become more and more like the new churches in their services. This is an overreaction to some of the problems of the past. First, it means effectively unchurching a great mass of people who cannot adjust to what they feel is an overemotional and subjective approach to worship. Second, it means abandoning a wonderful heritage of Spirit-filled hymns and music from earlier generations.

For me the goal is to combine a variety of the old and the new; the worship leader is like the scribe trained for the kingdom 'who brings out of his treasure what is new and what is old'.[26] One of the reasons why charismatic leaders have tended to favour non-liturgical services and the new music is because they have an eye to the future. They look at those Christians who bring their friends, those who are making disciples. It has certainly been my observation over the years that those church members who invite their neighbours are those who also worship most enthusiastically in the new ways. It is because they are in touch with newcomers and those who are unchurched that they are sensitive to what kind of worship will bring them into the kingdom.

But this is an oversimplification. There are still some quite large groups of people in parts of our society who, if they were to come to church, would connect most easily with the traditional service-shape and music. Even if the words have changed they know how to use written prayers and are accustomed to the inherited patterns of word and sacrament. Of course in some urban areas churches are situated so near to one another that one church can specialize in one kind of worship and its neighbours in another. In a town with ten churches offering traditional worship it is not unreasonable for the eleventh to offer worship in a freer, less liturgical style. But in churches where there are few convenient neighbours the balancing act becomes more difficult. There seem to be two ways of meeting this challenge with integrity. The first is to continue to wrestle with services which, over the course of a month, contain a balance of old and new music, form and freedom, objective and subjective worship. The second is to offer different services with different needs clearly in mind. Here are some examples.

Parish A is a small town where the church has outgrown its ancient building. There is a mix of formal and informal worship with a move over recent years in the direction of the informal. A new church centre has been opened on an estate at the opposite end of the parish from the medieval church. As planned, the new larger building has been the setting for a more self-consciously informal all-age service, aimed in particular at the people living on the estate. The old parish church has been left to the 'rump' of older people, the choir and others who protested against the new music. The new service is going well in the new building and relationships are being built with the estate. But, to the surprise of everyone, the numbers going to the traditional service in the old church have doubled, with many newcomers among them!

Parish B is an inner-city parish where a vast building houses a very small congregation at a relaxed Parish Communion. In the last two years a curate has started a lively new monthly 'Service of the Word', with baptism families and those unused to the liturgies of the church particularly in mind. The two key features have been the lay worship team, which has devised the highly imaginative content, and the multi-ethnic gospel choir. A whole new congregation has grown up.

Parish C is an urban/suburban parish which in the 1980s planted a new congregation in a school. Now that the main morning service in the parish church is full again, the vicar and PCC are planning to start a new 9 a.m. service and close the 8 a.m. early celebration. The new 9 a.m. will be a more formal Parish Communion with choir, hymns and a sermon. This will release the 11 a.m. to follow the desire of the majority for a more informal and less tightly structured time of worship.

Parish D is in a retirement area where a comfortable elderly congregation is growing at the mid-morning traditional service. However, there is a primary school in the parish and there are requests for baptism. The PCC recently appointed a youth and families worker who noticed that young parents loitered in the Sunday school rather than go back into church; she has started a separate 'satellite' family service in the church hall, which is increasingly popular.

All these examples arose from the experience of churches which discovered that there are many different people groups in our society, and some of them were effectively being excluded from Christian worship by the very worship that was designed to serve them. But in each case the desire to reach out and serve their community led to imaginative new worship, which created new congregations. Often the first step to the new congregation was the courage to break the stranglehold of the inherited pattern. One of the easiest ways to do this is to devise new services for special occasions. In our society where Sunday has become a crowded day for most people it is difficult for newcomers to imagine becoming committed to a weekly act of worship. But where churches regularly put on 'special' services, it is surprising how many new people come. The crib service, Mothering Sunday, harvest and Remembrance Sunday are the obvious occasions, but canny worship committees add local celebrations and anniversaries, invite uniformed and other local organizations, and often end up with a monthly service that forms the basis of a new congregation.

I am always grateful that at my theological college we students were allowed to devise fresh and experimental music at chapel instead of Mattins every Tuesday. Although the result was often painful, it taught us a great deal about the delights of creating imaginative offerings of worship in teams. Worship is too important to be left to the professionals. It also opened our eyes to some of the gifts needed for effective worship, and drove us back to our inherited liturgies with a vastly increased appreciation of them. Compared with our feeble efforts there were giants in the land in those days! If a parish is to be a centre for excellence in worship then lively and regular experiment will be part of our learning and growing.

Worship draws us out from our concerns to give ourselves to the Other. Where congregations are true to their biblical roots and true to their local communities, worship trains us to grow up in love and to make Christ's self-offering the centre and pattern of our lives.

4
Preaching – Handing on the Vision

WHY PREACH?

Preaching has such a bad name that it is sensible to ask why we do it. The very word has unfortunate overtones. When we say, 'Please don't preach at me!' we mean a kind of address that assumes an objectionably superior position, full of unwanted and insensitive advice, which is talking *at* rather than communicating *with*. No one wants to be preached at. A second reason for questioning the value of preaching is that it is, many people say, inherently boring. We live in a visual age and we are used to being entertained. In half an hour's television we are accustomed to plenty of action, excitement and humour. The credits after the programme tell us that dozens of people have laboured full-time with the latest technology and no expense spared to stop us from being bored. How can any local preacher compete? Third, it is often maintained that preaching is a poor way to communicate, let alone educate. We learn as we question, participate in, argue – not as we listen passively to a monologue.

Yet, contrary to this received wisdom, people travel miles to hear good preaching. Go to any popular Christian conference or holiday and you will see thousands of people listening hour after hour in rapt attention, as if their lives depended on it – which, in a sense, they do. Go to any growing church and you will almost always find preaching at the centre of that growth.

Preaching is not out of date in a visual age, though boring preaching certainly is. Now that we have to compete with television we cannot read out a learned treatise while the hourglass slowly empties, as they did when there was nothing better to do on the Sabbath than go to church; but we can give people what they desire even more than entertainment. The diva looks wonderful on the silver screen but in real life you can see the joins in her plastic surgery. What sportsman will watch at home when there is a chance to see the game live, or play oneself? In the same way the preacher who gives 'the words of life' will not go short of listeners. The church is healthier when we are sharpened up by a little competition from the mass media. People are soon wise to the fact that a visual age lacks depth.

If we are to see a new revival of faith in our time one of the most important ingredients will be a rediscovery of the power of preaching God's word to his people. This conviction has been challenged by Christian Schwarz's work on church growth.[1] In his stimulating study of 1,000 churches in 32 countries, Schwarz isolates eight features that characterize growing churches, and preaching (along with some other features that one might expect such as good youth and children's work and serious proportional giving) does not appear. For a book that purports to be about 'natural' church growth, it adopts a strangely programmatic approach, but it is nonetheless a very useful study; so why does it ignore preaching? The answer, according to some of the English popularisers of Schwarz, is that preaching is not significant. However, my own guess[2] is that, for a German Lutheran such as Schwarz, the category 'inspiring worship service', which is one of his eight 'quality principles', may well assume good preaching; in many Lutheran churches the sermon is in fact the main part of the worship. Whatever the truth, I continue to maintain that inspiring preaching is a vital foundation for a growing church and that its absence is a recipe for anaemic church life.

Preaching receives little serious attention in theological colleges and courses when you consider how much time will be given to it in the local church. I do not remember receiving any course of instruction at all on the subject in my own college. But I do remember the good preachers on the staff, and especially the Principal, Alec Motyer, who was exceptionally gifted; and I spent much time trying to work out why he was so inspiring. Part of the answer was his approach to Scripture.

CAN WE STILL USE THE BIBLE IN PREACHING?

It was fashionable a little while ago to assert that the cultural gap between Bible times and our own was so great that it was unbridgeable.[3] How, for example, can we begin to use the Bible when we teach on marriage from the pulpit? What connection is there between David and Solomon with their hundreds of wives and concubines and ourselves? How can anyone teach about homosexuality using the gang-rape episode in Genesis 19 about Sodom? Surely to jump from Bible times to our own in a sermon is to be guilty of a staggeringly naive kind of *mauvaise foi*.

This is a superficially attractive but deeply flawed view. First, there is a fundamental continuity in human nature, which instantly crosses the centuries. When I read of Hosea's lament about the unfaithfulness of his wife I could be in almost any street in this parish. When I read the psalmist's paranoid anxiety about his enemies I could be talking to a stressed executive in a multi-national. Simply on a human level the Bible is no more confined to its own time than Homer or Shakespeare. On the contrary our own history cannot be understood without seeing it shaped by the Bible, far more than by any other book. Second, cultural gaps are not a function of time alone. If I visit first a working-class family and then a professional family, I cross a cultural divide in one evening and in one parish; but we still communicate.

No, the subtext of the argument of those who wish to play down the use of the Bible is that we have lost our belief in the ability of God to reveal himself to us. It is God, after all, whose faithfulness enables us to be confident about any kind of knowing. He chooses to speak supernaturally through the Scriptures and we are foolish to ignore them, because it is through our Bible reading that we become acquainted with his ways. Since his character is constant, the God whom we learn about in the Scriptures is the same God who reveals himself today. If the link between Bible and Church is cut then the Church withers catastrophically. In fact a major cause of the present decline in the older denominations in the West is the loss of systematic biblical· preaching. If we pray for God to speak to our generation we will find that prayer being answered first of all through the Bible.

THE POINT OF PREACHING

What is the point of my next sermon? I could answer, 'I'm down to preach at 10 a.m., it's the Sunday after the Ascension, and I've got to say something to the Brownies.' This kind of response is perfectly understandable, but sets me off on quite the wrong tack. It leads me to concentrate on the task, on myself and the congregation; to be frank, it leads me to focus on acquitting myself favourably by finding something interesting to say. The task will take its place among all the other tasks of the week and will be done against a deadline. It will be treating the congregation as an audience. It will be a missed opportunity for the preacher and the congregation.

It is true that the congregation has not come to be bored, but nor has it come to be entertained. People have come to hear God's word. That means, not just timeless truths, but God speaking to us now through his word by the Spirit. If we are not able to say that just as God spoke clearly then, so similarly he speaks to us now through the Scriptures, we do our congregations a grave disservice.

How was it that Jesus spoke with authority? Not just because his sermons were good, though no doubt they were. Not just because his sermons were based on the Scriptures of his time, though they were.[4] He spoke with authority because he knew what he was talking about – God and his kingdom. When he preached he not only spoke but he did: he forgave sins, healed the sick, drove out demons and raised the dead. As John Wimber said, proclamation was linked to demonstration.[5]

Here at once is a difficulty for preachers. Perhaps one of the problems with charismatic renewal needs to be brought out into the open at this point. There is sometimes the unspoken implication that just around the corner (if only we prayed enough or believed enough) we too could demonstrate what we preach: we could preach about healing and then demonstrate it, preach about raising the dead and then show how it is done. But as far as one can tell that has never been a real possibility for preachers. Even those who claim more than most of us admit that. Oral Roberts, the famous US healing evangelist, once said, 'If I could heal when I wanted to, I would go round emptying the wards of our hospitals one by one. But I can't.'[6] And nor can anyone else.

Miracles certainly continue to happen, even in our tired and cynical Western culture; they include miracles of healing, as most

Christians can testify. But by definition 'miracle' is something out of the ordinary, exceptional. So Christian preaching cannot be a simple 'how to' story. There is a paradox here, a 'foolishness' in the preaching of the gospel, which is apparent to all who come to church. Christians are frequently disappointing and disappointed in our spiritual progress. Here, as with St Peter, 'is work in progress', not a finished product.

But that does not mean that we are let off the hook. Much public preaching has had a tendency in recent years to reduce itself to an extended 'thought for the day', modelling itself on articles in the serious press; and that will not do. There is more to preaching than a thoughtful essay or good advice; it has by definition to be gospel, good news. It has to proclaim and to demonstrate. And what can be demonstrated as well as proclaimed is that preaching the good news of Jesus changes individuals and builds communities. That is of course one of the things that the New Testament itself asserts. It was the preaching of the gospel that produced the new churches all round the shores of the Mediterranean in the first two centuries of the Christian era. We assume that preaching builds churches on the mission field.[7] But preaching comes alive in the 'settled' local congregation too when it becomes part of the process by which God builds up his church.

In particular, when the preacher expounds the Scripture and is able to say, like Peter, 'this is that which was spoken [of] by the prophet'[8] – that is, what we are experiencing now by the power of the Spirit is in continuity with what God did through Abraham and Moses and Nehemiah and Jesus and Paul, and all the generations between – then the sermon comes alive. It also becomes a corporate enterprise, even if apparently a monologue, as the congregation is inspired by this vision and people start to hear God's calling upon their own lives and commitments.

In times of renewal the spiritual temperature rises and Christians feel closer to the Acts of the Apostles and to the return of Christ. They see the church not as their Sunday morning habit or hobby but as part of God's great plan for the redemption of the world, and they come for teaching about their part in salvation history. Peter and the other apostles would not have achieved overmuch if, a week before Pentecost, they had advertised a sermon on the prophet Joel. After the Spirit fell on them, however, they knew, and 3,000 others knew, that the explanation of the meaning of their lives and the destiny of the world lay in the prophet Joel. In a similar way, when God moves by his Spirit in the local church, people come to understand how he moves by listening to Bible preaching.

In preaching, then, authority is focused not in the preacher alone, but in the way that Bible-plus-preaching-plus-congregational experience-plus-worship produce a kind of electricity together. At its best this process ignites Christian communities.

An important part of this collaboration is testimony. Preaching about the way that God can change our lives it is all the more effective if someone is in the position to stand up and say, in effect, 'Yes, it works! I know, because it has started to happen to me.' Of course much of the Spirit's work is slow and unseen. And when it is dramatic it is usually better not to shout about it, because pride has a way of coming before a fall. When God changes us in one part of our lives it often brings to light a problem in another. But it is healthy to celebrate that, in spite of the setbacks, God is alive and real and redeems vulnerable people like us. In this way preaching ultimately exalts God and his doings rather than the preacher.

LISTENING TO GOD

Is preaching the art of making a sermon and delivering it?
Why, no, that is not preaching. Preaching is the art of making
a preacher and delivering that!

Bishop William Quayle

The first stage in preparing a sermon is the most important and the most difficult to describe. It is starting to change my life to God's agenda by learning to listening to him. God speaks in dozens of different ways, and how he speaks depends partly on the way he has made us. Different members of the preaching team have different gifts for listening. But for the preacher the place to start is the daily reading and meditating upon Scripture. We cannot speak to others until we have learned for ourselves how

God speaks to us through his word. We cannot say anythir worthwhile until we have learned how to read, mark, learn and inwardly digest. How that reading–and–meditating becomes a two-way conversation is mysterious, but it does, and is of great value. A colleague makes a habit of unlocking the church doors some time before Morning Prayer and during the waiting time meditates on the Scripture passages for the day. During Mattins the word is read and worshipped. Then, he says, as he goes back for breakfast something from those Scriptures seems to become part of him, so that when it comes to preaching or doing a pastoral task, he already has something to say. Another friend says that he makes a practice of praying for the pastoral visits he is going to make; it is frequently his experience that things then happen during the visits which illuminate the passages of Scripture that he is study-ing for the following Sunday. As a result he is able to say from the pulpit, 'While I was visiting earlier in the week . . .' to illustrate the point.

The unceasing challenge which God puts before me is to change to his agenda. My inclination would be to dream up something to say on a Saturday, and to give to God (and to the congregation) the fag end of the week in preparation. His agenda is for me to be able to speak authoritatively about him, and about how knowing him has started to change even a stubborn and wayward heart like mine.[9] Waiting upon God takes time and effort but preaching out of the overflow of what God is doing in my life, in the lives of colleagues and friends, and in the church is much more exciting than working out what to say on my own! Over the years I have noted several components in my attempts to listen to God and understand his ways.

- The first component in listening to God is starting to change my life to his agenda, by expanding my prayer times, devel-oping a Bible reading plan and learning to listen to God and understand his purposes by study and meditation. Keeping a notebook soon results in ideas and discoveries that lead naturally into preaching.
- The second component for the regular preacher is to build a

small personal library of commentaries, study helps such as Bible handbooks, concordance, dictionaries and the like, and books that aid understanding of Christian doctrine, history and ethics. We owe it to our congregations to go on stretching our minds and our understanding. In the same way if we are going to have useful illustrations of how the Bible speaks then we will want to be reading biographies, missionary adventures, stories, histories – sacred and secular.

- Jesus said, 'Learn from me . . .' He taught his disciples by taking them with him. A major problem with the modern denominations is that they place a preacher alone in a congregation, often for years at a time without models. I have been particularly encouraged and helped, first by belonging to a preaching team who take notes and comment on one another's sermons, and second by going to see the kind of preachers that people turn out to listen to, and working out how they do it and what parts of their technique would be right for me to work at. It is not just the preacher that I analyse. The way that preacher and local church interact is also very instructive. The old Protestant preaching-house model is good for babes in Christ but not for producing people who will make disciples.

- You cannot turn other people into travellers if you present yourself as having arrived. A fellow traveller who knows the problems of the way is of more use than someone offering advice from a map.

- But the Christian life is not just about travelling; it is also about going on being converted. If we are to help others change we have to be being changed in such a way that sometimes others can see how it happens and how it feels. Many preachers develop a protective shell because we have been hurt over the years or pushed around by congregations. The result is not only poverty of spirit for ourselves but sermons that may be superbly polished but somehow do not touch hearts. To allow the Spirit to call us by name and open us up again is a deeply healing and refreshing experience for ourselves and it enables heart to touch heart in our preaching.

The journalist Bernard Levin once said that producing his regular columns for *The Times* was like being hit by the sails of a windmill. The moment you had recovered from one the next bore down upon you. Certainly the weekly sermons are a constant pressure. But if you are taking in and drinking from God's well, then it becomes a delight to preach. Psalm 84.5–6 in the Book of Common Prayer puts it well: 'Blessed is the man whose strength is in thee: in whose heart are thy ways. Who going through the vale of misery use it for a well: and the pools are filled with water.' What starts out as a burdensome yoke becomes light and easy – a duty and a joy.

PUTTING IT INTO PRACTICE

There are several different kinds of starting points and subject matter for preaching: ethical, social and doctrinal questions, apologetic and evangelistic themes, devotional and spirituality questions, teaching about worship and the nature of the Church. But the bread and butter of Christian preaching is (or should be) an opening up of the Scriptures for the day. To say this is controversial, because in many churches it does not happen and in most theological colleges it is not taught. But until the end of the eighteenth century a regular diet of sermons consisting of the exposition of Scripture was the universal expectation of the Church in England and Europe. Since Vatican II a homily on the Gospel for the day has been the usual practice of the Roman Church; indeed the 'primary duty' of the clergy: 'Thus they establish and build up the people of God.'[10] It is time that the rest of us got back to what is the most effective way of feeding a congregation and enabling it to grow.

Expository preaching seeks to bring God's living word to a congregation by starting from the study of a biblical passage or unit of text. There are gifted preachers who start with a verse or even a single word and preach effective sermons; but this denies a congregation the excitement of seeing how the biblical writer develops a theme. No, real Christian preaching starts normally with a unit of text – a parable, an incident, a passage of teaching – lays it out in front of the worshippers and invites them to enter the gospel behind the words. When a congregation has Bibles open and follows a text being read, expounded and applied, there is a special kind of silence, of being in the presence of the God who speaks, which impresses even the cynic. It is a common experience for someone to go to a service as a visitor, to hear expository preaching for the first time and to say to the preacher something like, 'I've been looking for this all my life. I felt while you were speaking that God was speaking to me, and I must respond.'

CHOOSING THE PASSAGE

For many preachers the selection of the Scripture passage is done for us. Anglicans, for instance, have a lectionary that follows a three-year cycle of several readings per Sunday, so there is both a framework and freedom of choice. There is a sense of community in knowing that congregations all over the country will be looking at the same Scriptures; and having set readings avoids the danger of a preacher choosing topics that reflect private preferences or eccentric doctrines. A breakthrough in our own church happened when we decided to link the Sunday morning sermon series with the housegroup themes. Each quarter there is a sense of purpose and growing excitement as the whole congregation finds itself discovering what the Spirit is saying to the church through a particular book of the Bible.

GETTING STARTED

The next stages in sermon preparation are not easy to describe without making them sound mechanical. These days sermon ideas usually 'just come'. But there was a time, because I had never been taught how to preach, when I thrashed around for days wondering what on earth to say. Learning a system step by step seems an odd thing to do but once it has been learned it can be adapted and changed. Here is the method that I have found most useful, broken down into steps.

STAGE 1: STUDYING THE PASSAGE

The aim is to see what the passage is about. Read the passage through prayerfully several times in different translations until you get the feel of it. Note down what it seems to be about.

Then read round the passage to discover the context. It is unwise, for instance, to expound Romans 13, about every person being subject to the governing authorities, without seeing that it is a subsection of Romans 12, which begins with the call not to be conformed to this world but to be transformed. In other words what in Romans 13 looks like a call to conformity is in context a concession or an exception to a call to revolution.

Next note down what the author's intentions appear to be and how he or she is communicating them. Obviously there are many different genres in the Bible. An Epistle is quite different from a Gospel or the Acts. One of the reasons why expository preaching fell out of favour is that preachers tended to treat every text in the same way, with the result that all the Bible's different styles became flattened into one 'religious' language, which had more to do with the culture of the preacher than that of the passage.

It is at this stage, after prayerfully studying the passage on your own and noting down initial thoughts, that a commentary can be useful. Often New Testament passages have Old Testament texts in view to a far greater extent that we realize. For instance we cannot explain John 1.43–51 (the call of Nathanael, an Israelite without guile) without understanding the several nuanced references to Genesis 27 and his forefather Jacob who had plenty of guile.

The aim of this stage is to be able to say what the main theme or central idea of the passage is. As Haddon Robinson points out in his classic on preaching[11] this is worth practising. For instance, James 1.5–8 (RSV): 'If any of you lacks wisdom, let him ask God, who gives to all men generously and without reproaching, and it will be given him . . .' At first sight you might say that this passage is about *wisdom*. That is true, but too broad – we are not told much about wisdom here. A little more thought will produce more precision: the passage is about *how to get wisdom*. And a glance at the context will show that it is about *how to get wisdom when you are facing pressure*.[12] Finally, it is no good saying what a text is about unless you can also say what the author is saying about his subject. In this instance, the author is saying, *If you want to know how to get wisdom in times of pressure*, then *ask God for it*.

It is worth doing this apparently artificial kind of exercise if only because of the way in which the Scriptures keep on surprising. For instance the parable of the Good Samaritan appears to be about being a good neighbour. The text moves towards the injunction, 'Go and do likewise', and one hears numerous talks about how it is important to be a good neighbour, which is unexceptionable but extremely dull. Why should such a dull story be so well known?

The parable of the Good Samaritan is actually an exercise in conversion by surprise. A lawyer who thinks he knows his law tries to justify himself (a dangerous thing to do in the presence of Christ). So Jesus tells a story that is almost certainly meant to be about the lawyer himself, which must have amused the crowd and, in so doing, requires him to imagine himself needing help, being robbed and injured and then being unable to be over-particular about what kind of neighbour would help him.[13] Presumably the lawyer wanted to push Jesus into the corner of admitting that he was not being as strict on sinners as the law demanded. Instead he finds Jesus (with a great deal of humour which is hidden by the centuries and the translation) pushing him into a corner where his question is turned upside down.

It is in fact the classic piece of teaching against patronizing do-goodery, and asserts the good news that in Jesus we who are lamed by life receive a blank cheque from him for recovery. When we are thus converted and have received from him, then, and only then, are we commanded to go out and do likewise. This parable will be preached many times over the years, and each time the great reversal will be fresh. There are so many different levels and angles to the Scripture that all sorts of different sermons can be produced. But the key will be where the listeners are. Do they naturally identify more with the lawyer, or with the Samaritan, or with the man who was mugged?[14]

STAGE 2: SO WHAT?

The next stage is move from the text to the sermon. The main idea(s) of the text will be related to the main theme of the sermon but they are unlikely to be identical. Much so-called expository preaching lets itself down badly at this point by a superficial sliding over this stage. For instance, if an expository sermon *explains* a parable, it may well be doing the very opposite of what

Jesus intended! If Jesus had intended to teach three things about God beginning with P he would surely have done so. To reduce a parable to this is to empty it of its converting power. Once the preacher in his study has understood something of the original impact of the story and (for example) the three things about God that lie behind that, the next task is to ask what the Spirit might be wanting to say to the church next week and whether some story, dialogue or dramatic sketch might not be the best way of doing it.

For preaching to be effective the preacher will acquire the habit of having multi-level conversations, of inhabiting several worlds at once – the cultures of the Bible, the Christian tradition, current affairs, local history, the congregation's growth and development – and of hearing the voice of the Spirit saying how the passage might relate to all these different things. The idea(s) of the sermon will be a development of the main idea(s) of the text, and will arise out of the text but also out of the conversation between God, the preacher and the various other players noted above.

For example the main idea of John 1.43–51 (the call of Nathanael) might be that Jesus reveals himself as the true Israel and his role as the ladder between earth and heaven. The main idea of a sermon on the passage might be 'how to open heaven to a friend'.

So-called biblical preaching can be extremely dull if it is simply a re-exposition of the original text. Paul's letters in particular suffer from this treatment. A series of sermons on, say, Romans, can start by analysing each paragraph and breaking it down into logical points, which are then presented to the long-suffering congregation. Even the most patient church will get bored towards the end, however worthy the aim.[15]

This way of handling texts is not what we find in the Bible itself. The apostles, like the Lord himself, seem to have meditated on the sacred words of the Old Testament and to have chewed them over until they made them their own, and then regurgitated them in a new, relevant and Spirit-filled form, like Ezekiel in his calling.[16] The Beatitudes, for instance, are clearly a reworking of Old Testament themes; none of them is without Old Testament foundation or provenance, but they are produced in such a way as to make them new and astonishing. This is how the old word becomes new, and how the new preaching impresses itself as being full of authority. This is the preacher turned prophet. In practice the preacher who chews over a text and absorbs it after listening to God and the world will often find better ways of presenting the text than simply analysing or re-presenting it with a commentary. Maybe a particular theme or sub-theme will be the one to emphasize on this occasion. Maybe a sideline in the text will be a pointer to a major theme in the rest of Scripture or a moral issue in the newspapers this week. The more one practises, the more imaginative and less wooden the re-presenting of Scripture from the pulpit becomes.

There are many different ways of making an imaginative leap from the main idea of the text to the main idea of the sermon. I am grateful to see how very different the preaching is when done by different members of our preaching team. My own tendency has been to use a logical framework with two or three main points and some sub-headings. But I have noticed frequently how much I enjoy and profit from preaching by my colleagues that follows the logic of the story rather than that of the lecture room and use the windows of the visual imagination rather than those of the deductive process to inspire and envision.

For example if I were preaching on John 20.19–23 about Jesus' sudden appearance through locked doors in the upper room on the first Easter Day, I would be inclined to dwell on the fact of the resurrection, the kind of peace which the risen Lord brings, and the commissioning of the disciples through a proleptic experience of the Spirit. One of my colleagues, however, would probably start in a much more imaginative way. She might talk about the fact that although the disciples were nominally in the place of faith, the upper room, their minds were elsewhere, wondering what the Jewish authorities were planning, and the doors to the upper room were locked because of their fears. We too, she might continue, are gathered in the place of faith, our church, but for many of us our minds are elsewhere; we have doubts and fears and worries that we do not bring into the open but are preoccupying us just the same. And there are plenty of locked doors on the route to our hearts. But closed doors are no barrier to the risen Lord who understands where we are. Just as he turned those apostles round from being frightened and withdrawn from the world into ambassadors of his peace to the world so the risen Jesus can do that for his Church now. This kind of approach can be more effective than a coldly logical one, and is more in tune with the way in which the early Church used the Old Testament.

Even more important, though, than the particular method we use to move from text to sermon is the sense of what God might be wanting to say to his people this week through the ancient text. Of course this is not a separate stage in producing a sermon, but equally it is not one that can be left out. It seems to me that the way that the early Church preached was heavily dependent upon the Old Testament and yet also quite independent of it. The apostles had so thoroughly digested the sacred text and pondered its fulfilment in the Age of the Spirit that they were able to re-present it in a way that was new, inspiring and authoritative, and 'not as the scribes', who presumably used the old teaching methods of the schools of the Pharisees. The shock to their audiences was that here were unschooled people producing the word of God in a way that touched hearts and minds and changed them.[17] The reason was that they had spent time with Jesus. That is also our aim before saying anything.

If, though, listening to the Spirit is fundamental in preaching, is there still a place for carefully ordered preparation of the kind outlined here? Very much so. In fact it is in drawing these two together that a properly Trinitarian ministry of preaching under the authority of the Father can take place.

STAGE 3: CONSTRUCTING A SERMON WITH A PURPOSE

The next stage is to work on the main purpose of the sermon and how to achieve it. A poor aim would be 'To preach a good sermon on 2 Corinthians 9'. A better aim might be 'To expound 2 Corinthians 9 in such a way as to inspire the congregation about the joys of Christian giving'. An even better one might be 'To raise giving and for the congregation to enjoy doing it'.

The question is how to construct the sermon to achieve the purpose. Different structures work differently. A structure that looks simple on paper, with headings, sub-headings and a developing argument, can be very difficult to listen to without the notes. A more informal structure – where the same point is made, illustrated and applied before moving on to the next point – can work better. Some preachers like to produce spidergrams to help them create an unfolding story or dialogue.

STAGE 4: ILLUSTRATING FOR A VISUAL AGE

When you are part of a congregation you become aware that people start to fidget during long sessions of theologizing, however worthy. Our capacity for straight doctrine or exposition of Scripture is quite limited and our attention span is very short. On the other hand our capacity for stories seems unlimited. The preacher can harness this just as Jesus did. There are many reasons why good conference speakers can hold our attention for 40 or 50 minutes, but one reason is that they make their points come alive by illustrating them. Of course there is a danger here, as the old divines were fond of pointing out. It is possible to make the sermon serve the anecdotes rather than the other way round. But it need not be so!

Illustrations provide a breather for the concentration, like a natural break in a television programme. They set the imagination free and touch the heart and will as well as the brain. They provide a concrete way of understanding difficult concepts. Parables come alive with modern equivalents, like the true story of the young pimp at the beginning of *The Father Heart of God*,[18] which movingly re-enacts the return of the Prodigal Son, and illustrates what repentance feels like.

It is a useful discipline to try to illustrate and apply each main point of a sermon; first, because it helps the listeners and, second, because it keeps the preacher in check and makes sure that the content is relevant. To this end I have found it useful to have a sermon-planner: a sheet on which I can sketch out the main structure and ideas of the sermon with the illustrations and applications. Of course I do not do it mechanically, or using the same structure each time. But it prevents me from rambling or from having no coherent plan at all.

Illustrations need not just be verbal ones, of course. A picture on a screen can be worth a thousand words. But it is only half-illustrated if all you put up on the screen is more words! A well-illustrated sermon can be particularly useful for all-age worship. I often tell a Bible story using cartoons and keep up a patter that is aimed both at the children and also at the adults. Sometimes I notice that these simple sermons are more effective in teaching the adults deep Christian truths than my longer and more thoughtful ones for adults only.

CONCLUSIONS

Where does the sermon go in the end? The honest answer, often enough, is nowhere. It does not matter if two days later people do not remember the points of the sermon. But what does matter is where we are taking people and for what purpose. A sermon will have a general aim: for instance, a sermon on Matthew 6.29 (RSV: 'even Solomon in all his glory was not arrayed like one of these') might have the aim of encouraging the poor and insignificant followers of Jesus to live like kings and priests.[19] But it should also take the hearers somewhere definite at its conclusion. If preaching is part of worship then giving people the chance to respond is important. When the service is Holy Communion then the walk up to take the sacrament can focus the response: 'As we come up to receive the life of Christ again, let us gratefully. . .' Otherwise there will need to be a pause for prayer, for commitment, for resolve. If there is a team prepared to pray at the end of the service then people can be directed to them. Perhaps we preachers should not be surprised that our listeners do want to respond to sermons – but a clear ending is needed.

THE IMPORTANCE OF PREACHING

I have tried to argue that preaching is vital to healthy congregations. It is only one part of the formation of Christians, of course. But it is a vital part. In an act of worship the sermon gathers the various parts of the liturgy together. At its best it will inspire and convert. A church is held together by a common vision, and that vision will be transferred to worshippers most often and effectively by preaching. Of course our preaching is always provisional; most

5
Making Disciples

Go therefore and make disciples . . .
Matthew 28.19

ONE-DAY-A-WEEK CHRISTIANS?

However inspiring the preaching is on Sunday, it does not make much of a dent on Monday to Saturday. One of the undoubted causes of weakness in the churches is the idea that attendance at a service once a week can build disciples – the kind of Christians who will be able to make a difference in the world. It will not normally work; because, unless the Sunday congregation is very small and the service is very informal, there is no opportunity for the Christians to ask questions, report back or be trained. No one could train bricklayers by instructing them for ten minutes a week from a 25m distance. Much less so can one make Christians. Being a disciple is a growing and learning process. Therefore that growth and that learning have to take place, and a local church must have a strategy. This will have several strands. The first has to do with growth in knowledge of the faith; the second with applying this to one's place of work and one's home. Each feeds the other. A third relates both to building a climate of expectation that Christians are people who learn and develop and to providing clear models. A fourth will enable growing Christians to develop ministries and give out to others what they have received.

I grew up with the pastoral presumption of the Church of England that most English people were more or less Christians and simply needed to be reminded of that from time to time. It was important to invite people to come to church but exceedingly bad manners to enquire into their souls. If they became regular communicants then it was up to God to nourish them further. But I kept meeting Christians from other backgrounds and other countries who took training seriously – and seemed to know how to disciple others rather more successfully than we did. Many excellent Christian leaders in the Anglican Church had their initial training in Methodist youth clubs or interdenominational camps where young leaders could practise their skills.

A growing Christian needs more than a Sunday service. A Christian who will be able to pass on his or her faith to the next generation has to have at least two 'networks for growth'. The first will be a personal network, perhaps a prayer partnership of just one or two friends. This is the equivalent to the intimate circle of three or four disciples whom Jesus often took with him on training exercises. The second network will be a housegroup or cell of eight to 15 people. In addition most Christians will want to join specific training courses from time to time, or specific interest groups to help apply their faith to their particular profession or life situation. Perhaps it is helpful to outline the scope of each of these networks for our formation in Christ.

PRAYER PARTNERS

I have valued greatly belonging to a small group of 'prayer partners' and have encouraged others to try it over the years, so that now in our church quite a large proportion of the members belong to a partnership. Many of them began as 'prayer triplets' in preparation for Mission England. These prayer triplets had the specific purpose of praying for non-Christian friends. In the one to which I belonged, we had the joy of seeing one man we prayed for come to church with his wife straightaway, and another was converted after several months of prayer. My own particular group of prayer partners has grown to five and will probably split when it becomes six. We meet at a time convenient to us (Wednesday 7 to 7.30 a.m.); we take it in turn to lead by reading a verse or two from the Bible and commenting upon it, and then we turn to prayer, both for one another – our work, our families, our needs and our problems – and for a small list of friends who, we are praying, will turn to Christ. It is an effort to get there on winter mornings, but we continue to be surprised at the numbers of answers to prayer that we receive and to be encouraged by the mutual support through our problems and life crises. Many of us find personal prayer difficult, but much easier with the regular encouragement of a small group of friends with whom one can share.

HOUSEGROUPS

Most growing churches have housegroups or something similar. In order to develop as Christians we all need a group to belong to that is smaller and more intimate than the congregation. In our increasingly anonymous and individualistic society it is good to belong to a 'little flock' where we can practise our faith, ask our questions, share our doubts and build relationships. The Christian life is a *koinonia* – a life lived in common; to pray '. . . and the fellowship of the Holy Spirit be with us all' without structuring a network of discipleship groups into our churches is a contradiction.

The objective side of the housegroup meetings is a Bible study, and the key strategic decision in our church has been to link the study with the Sunday sermon series. The mid-week housegroup and Sunday sermon reinforce each other and enlarge the opportunity for discovering and learning. Each term we produce our own booklet of material with questions for discussion and prompts for prayer and action. Usually several people write one or two studies each and group members sometimes play the source-critical game of trying to guess who is behind this week's questions!

But 'Bible study' is a title that could give a wrong impression of our groups, which try to combine theory and practice. For instance if the passage is about Jesus' teaching on 'turning the other cheek', people will have many individual questions, which cannot be answered from the pulpit. 'My child is being bullied in school; should I teach her to stand up for herself, or what?' These questions can be worked at together in the small group, so that a community ethic, obedient to the gospel and sensitive to today's context, can evolve. 'Bible obedience groups' is more like it than 'Bible study', because our conviction is that when the Bible is opened among Christians, the Holy Spirit builds community. These are the 'base community groups' of South America, or the Methodist class groups of the eighteenth-century revival, transposed to the semi-pagan culture of the modern UK. Some churches go so far as to insist that their church *is* small groups meeting mid-week, and the Sunday combined gathering is more of an extra. After all, taking part in a small group is a more active commitment in some ways than 'going to church'. Over and over again our experience has been that, as congregations have grown, the quality of small-group life feeds into Sunday worship. If people come together on Sunday having something to sing about, it shows. Not of course that other parts of the week are excluded; but, if people are learning and doing in groups, it shows up and makes services come alive.

Most housegroups these days start with a welcome and time of worship, go into a period of reading and study, then move into a time of prayer and ministry, in which people can be prayed for. Small groups are good for learning to minister to one another, learning to practise spiritual gifts; they earth the faith and give Christians a set of relationships to grow into.

Leadership is vital to the success of housegroups. In some groups several people are capable of leading the 'study'; in others only one or two. But if groups are not to stagnate then strong, humble, patient and inspiring leadership is called for. One of my mistakes has often been to neglect the encouragement and nurture of group leaders. If people are going to lead groups effectively then they in their turn need much time. Otherwise they will be overwhelmed by the group, or turn the group meetings into formal, school-room sessions in which members neither grow nor experience the power of the Spirit.

Another essential for groups is a sense of progress. A group that is only a discussion group has a short life. Real Christianity of its very nature is always spilling over into service and evangelism in the community; a group of Christians meeting together should expect to have a powerful effect for good in the locality, and this will in turn commend the faith to neighbours. Of course in practice things are not always so simple. Half the group may be struggling with their own problems, which absorb much of the leadership's energies. After two or three years it is likely that members will be so used to one another's opinions that a group will become tired and need some fresh approach. In some churches this is organized and people swap groups after every two years, which has the advantage of large numbers of people being introduced to one another. It is better still if growth means groups have to split and recombine.

Housegroups continue to flourish only if they have a clear purpose beyond themselves. Just as Christian marriage is ultimately about procreation or building community beyond the needs of the couple, so housegroups will have aims that encompass people who do not yet belong, projects in the wider world, acts of service in the local community, and ministries in the church.

DEVELOPING A MID-WEEK PROGRAMME

Different churches adopt different patterns of mid-week meetings. In one parish there was a local habit of attending the adult education centre for learning and so it was logical for the church to produce a 'Christian night school'. Most churches find that a period of coming together in larger meetings than housegroups can be beneficial as part of the pattern. A few years ago in our parish the demand grew for longer periods of teaching or more concentrated periods of worship and of waiting corporately in silence upon God than was possible on Sundays, and we started 'Thursday Special' on the first Thursday of each month. Our pattern was the first week all together and then three weeks in housegroups. We discovered that people are more committed to small groups than the larger gathering, but Thursday Special has grown and we have found it good for communicating a vision for new developments, for sustained teaching on controversial topics and for open prayer and ministry.

More recently we decided to adopt the pattern of some larger churches, which have two-tier group meetings. This is an attempt to grow more leaders and to expand the housegroup networks. It took a little while to organize and to iron out the teething problems, but we soon began to see some major benefits. On the first week of the month (Thursday Special) the whole church meets for worship, teaching and prayer; we try to give a 'vision' for the month. The second and fourth week of the month is for small groups or cells. These are like the old housegroups except that they are meant to be smaller and more intimate, with eight to ten people. They are still first and foremost 'Bible obedience groups', but the emphasis is different: the teaching is shorter and simpler; often the second meeting of the month will be putting the teaching into action. The stress is on sharing our lives, caring for one another, praying for one another. The third week of the month is for combined groups or 'pastorates', with 30 to 40 people and four to five groups. These groups are the workshops of the church – large enough for lively worship and ministry and having as their aim the carrying forward of the teaching or vision for the month. They are also the right size for many practical tasks and for hospitality.

The advantages of this new system are many. The cell-group leaders have a less exhausting task, being responsible only once a fortnight for their group. The church leader has shared the pastoral care of the cell-group leaders. Whereas I used to feel guilty that I was not regularly visiting the 25 or so leaders and deputies, now I have a manageable group of 'pastorate' leaders, who each have three or four cell-group leaders to care for. People who may have gifts for teaching or leading worship can be trained and tried out in a group appropriate to their experience. Someone who can play a guitar well in a cell group can be invited to lead worship in a pastorate, for instance. Already this has proved a useful training ground.

Although the system appears complicated it has produced more growth and strangely has resulted in a greater sense of cohesion. More people are involved in leadership and therefore 'own' the church vision. More people are doing the teaching and therefore more are learning.

Of course how a church divides itself up into groups will depend on many different factors. Several churches are trying out variations of 'cells' and similar developments.[1] But the principle that humans relate to one another naturally in different size groups and that Christians need to belong to more than the Sunday assembly to grow and be nurtured is important. It is not true that those who belong to mid-week groups withdraw from the world and care only for religious meetings; on the contrary a well-balanced mid-week programme will help Christians to grow in confidence in being witnesses at their place of work and will enable them to become more rounded human beings. When a congregation is discovering how God can move in their lives during the week then the Sunday services become deeply celebra- tory, and the great saving acts of Christ that we proclaim on the first day of the week speak of the richness of his provision on the other six. Nor is it true that this is a model of church that suits only comfortable suburban churches. While the pattern and organization of mid-week meetings will vary in different kinds of community, the principle that we Christians need to be discipled together is universal.

NEW CHRISTIANS AS DISCIPLES

James was a young farmer who was brought by a friend to one of our supper parties with a speaker. He was intrigued, then inter- ested, and finally convinced. It was exciting to see him lit up by the love of God and start to come to church. But from Monday to Saturday the old way of life kept reasserting itself; he did not know how to pray, his Bible reading was boring; he soon started to be absent on Sundays. When he did come there was a puzzled look on his face, as if to say, 'It seems to make sense when I come here, but I can't keep it up during the week.'

Special opportunities are needed for new Christians or those wanting a refresher course. One of the peculiarities of our post- Christian society in the West is that people have very different amounts of teaching about Christ and very different experience of the living Church. Some people come to us who know a consider- able amount about Christ but have as yet had no experience of a relationship with him; others are for all practical purposes pagans. For both these sorts of person (and for many others besides) 'church' is probably just not an option. So, like many others, we have devised or adapted suitable 'ways in' so that new people can learn about God's love for them in a way that will make sense for them.

For many years I have been offering a short course for enquirers about the Christian faith. It is particularly aimed at adults who do not quite know where they stand but are interested to discover more about God. It has had varied titles and content according to the needs of the times. The course has two sides to it, theoretical and experiential. So, for instance, Session 1 often asks the question, 'Does God exist and how can I know?' It tackles the popular notion still current in parts of our culture that science has disproved religion, so that faith is about the private and irrational side of life. It tackles the issues first by a re-statement of some of the arguments that show that science and Christianity are not mortal enemies, and second by using Scripture and personal stories to show how a sceptic can reach out to God and discover that he is there and waiting to get in touch. It is exciting to have a room full of adults, some of them agnostics and even atheists, all asking difficult questions, and it is thrilling when after four or five sessions some of them ask Jesus into their lives.

When Billy Graham first came to England he was able to address a generation who had mostly been to Sunday school and had Scripture lessons throughout their school years. Today similar young adults may well know more about the significance of Hindu festivals or their horoscope than about Good Friday. A young mother enquired about baptism recently and I asked her when was the last time she had heard about Jesus Christ. She said it was at school when she was about 11 years old when the teacher had told them that he was dead! Just as St Paul spent extended periods of time in the cities he visited on his missionary journeys, so churches in the West today are discovering the benefits of spending time with people, giving them opportunity to ask difficult questions, so that when the moment comes they will be able to make an informed decision.

Inevitably we have been influenced in recent years by the phenomenal success of the Alpha course run by Holy Trinity, Brompton, and have both used the Alpha course and gratefully adapted some of its features – such as inviting people to a meal – to our own courses. 'HTB' have a great gift of making the Christian faith simple (without being simplistic) and real in the sense that every point can be illustrated with true stories from people's lives. In particular they have taught me to be less reticent about the importance of showing people not only how to have a real relationship with their heavenly Father through Christ, but also how to experience the power of the Holy Spirit. The high

point of the Alpha course is when people go away for a weekend
course on the Spirit and spend time with God. People in our area
are less likely to be able to manage a weekend away, so we have a
Saturday away, and very moving it is to see the changes in people's
lives that stem from that. Here are a couple of sample letters I have
received:

> I have felt quite overwhelmed by our day away together last
> Saturday. I cannot begin adequately to thank you for giving me
> such an opportunity to learn so much of such essential signifi-
> cance to our lives . . . In fact since Saturday I have thought of
> nothing else and realize now how so many of the points and
> issues raised during the course from week to week have struck
> home.

> Although I felt touched on an earlier occasion by the Holy
> Spirit, part of me has always held back. Outward emotions have
> been hard to show. I very much try to put on a good front,
> always the coper, the jolly happy person. I came to the Saturday
> morning talk in my normal role of observer – 'This is for some-
> one else, not me' – but during the morning I increasingly felt
> this was for me and when the time came to ask the Holy Spirit
> to come to us I felt the anger and bitterness inside me so strong
> that I must do something about it, and when you and N asked
> to pray with me I felt I must give myself completely. As you
> asked for the anger and bitterness to leave, all these long-held
> emotions came rising to the surface, up and up until I thought
> I would explode, then nothing, absolutely nothing. I felt fright-
> ened till I realized they were going and I was left empty. I then
> let the Holy Spirit fill me with his love and peace and for the
> first time I felt complete as God meant me to be.

One year we had a rest from the usual housegroup programme
and invited the whole church to join our 'Baseline Course'. It was
shortly after we had built our new extension; as we gathered the
group leaders together to pray for it, one of them said, 'I believe
that God wants us to pray for 120 people to come to the basics

course.' Since we rarely had more than 50 to 60 for Thursday Specials I thought this was foolish, but as the new space we were to meet in was already called 'The Upper Room' the number 120 did seem appropriate. In fact 119 people came the first night and more the next. Church people brought friends and we had several new members as a result. More important I guess, however, will prove to be the impact on many of our older church members who have been coming Sunday by Sunday for years and (as can often happen with Anglicans) had never actually participated in a course of adult instruction in the Christian faith. For some of them it has been like a new spring-time.

Among the other helpful courses that have been devised in recent years, it is worth mentioning Emmaus and the adult catechumenate movement, which have been good at building community from new Christians, because ordinary Christians accompany the new members and act as sponsors or 'godparents' to the enquirers.[2] Sometimes people are keen to learn about the Christian faith but unable or unwilling to come to a course with others. For instance, a couple with young children who are enquiring about baptism may not be able to afford babysitters. In this case we offer them a similar course, but in their own home. We have not found anything better than the *Good News Down the Street* course by Michael Wooderson.[3] The special feature of this course is that it is taken by largely 'untrained' lay people who make themselves available to go to a neighbour's house and lead them through a simple course, which allows them to ask all the questions they want and ends with them being able to make a commitment to Christ. It not only results in people becoming Christian disciples but also helps church members to learn how to make disciples. Often someone who has asked for a *Good News Down the Street* course one year will be a helper on a team the next.

New Christians also benefit enormously from some individual attention. After making a commitment they meet for about an hour once a week or fortnight with a more experienced Christian normally of the same age, sex and interests. Part of that time will be spent in going through a short course on the faith; part will be a practical training in prayer and discipleship, learning to listen to God and see him act in their life.

The phone rang on early on Monday: 'I've been waiting since before 7 o'clock to tell you,' said the woman.

I came to the 11 o'clock service yesterday, and God spoke to me in a way he's never spoken before. I didn't know he could be so real. I didn't know he loved everyone. The sermon seemed just for me; the hymns were him getting in touch with me. I came back to the evening service and it happened again. I went to bed with my head buzzing, and when I woke up this morning he's still here with me. It's so wonderful I just had to tell you!

This young woman had first come to church through a baptism enquiry for her children. Then she had come fairly regularly to a Christian basics course with a friend and had made a commitment at the end of it. The two of them volunteered to restart a parent and toddler group, which has flourished. One of our leaders had noticed a few months later that both of them were drifting and starting to look puzzled when other people had spoken of their Christian experience. She invited them home one afternoon and went over the basics of the faith again, at the end of which they both made a more formal commitment of repentance and faith, and she prayed for them to be filled with the Spirit. She also arranged for another young mum to see them both once a week to do a one-to-one (or in this case one-to-two) course. The woman who phoned me said how helpful it was to be able to ask all the questions and have them answered properly. Some two years later her husband found Christ for himself.

Stories like these emphasize that in a post-Christian society, where knowledge of the faith and Christian friendships cannot be taken for granted, people need time to make commitment, time for it to become real in their lives, and proper nurture and loving care for them to make progress in the vital early years of discipleship. These two women want now to tell people what has happened to them – indeed it will be difficult to stop them telling the world. It is a wonderful gift to us of a healthy Christian birth. But it is also a reminder that many of our new Christians drift away or develop half-Christian habits and thinking, and are unable then to pass on the faith. A useful word from other training disciplines is 'mentor'. More and more we are discovering that new Christians flounder if they do not have a whole network of encouragements, among which is a special friend or mentor whose responsibility it is to care for their spiritual growth.

Another group in our church who plainly needed help was the younger men. Whereas the women seemed to get to know each other easily, the men found it difficult to make friends, and were slow to develop in their faith. One of the responses to this was to start a men's prayer breakfast which met from 7 to 9 a.m. each Saturday for food, Bible teaching and prayer. In effect it became a men's discipling group. The gifted lay leader drew the men out of themselves and helped them to grow in faith. In our society, women seem to be able to voice what is going on inside them and to form relationships easily, but men have much more difficulty. Particularly in church, men nod at one another but often do not progress beyond that. After a few weeks of the prayer breakfast it was difficult to stop the men from talking, and new natural friendships were being formed that strengthened the whole church. We prayed for one another, supported one another through various crises and generally started to relate as Christians. As a result the men have grown in confidence and faith and have started to show the leadership gifts and desire to pray that we have long seen in the women of our church.

PRODUCING THE VOLUNTEERS

Being a church leader in England is becoming more and more like being a pioneer missionary: there may not be anyone there to help, and clergy often swap stories of turning up at country churches and having to find the key, give out the hymn books, play the organ and count the collection as well as take the service. More serious is the situation of those ministers who feel themselves to be alone in a struggling church. A Pentecostal minister I know has to be the treasurer of the church and lead every aspect of its ministry; he feels himself to be completely alone.

Because family life has changed so much in the last generation, the general perception is that the number of people who have time to offer to the local church has fallen drastically. Far fewer women are at home during the day; paid work has become much more demanding; much energy is devoted each weekend to travelling to grandparents and separated parents. Of course this gloomy picture is not the whole truth. Although the great dreams of increased leisure, brought about by technology, have so far proved delusory, it is true that working hours for the average working person have dropped significantly over the last century and a half. Also the number of younger retired people has grown significantly. There is out there an untapped reservoir of man- and woman-power for the church to exploit. However, the experience of the clergy that it is becoming more difficult to recruit people remains valid. There are no easy short cuts to producing volunteers to staff a growing church, but there are some steps which most churches that have made progress in staffing have taken.

WAITING FOR THE VISION

Paradoxically the problem of the shortage of volunteers is at least as much a discipling problem as a personnel problem. If a church learns how to search out and make disciples, it will find an abundance of willing servants.[4]

PRAYING THEM IN

'The harvest is plentiful, but the labourers are few; pray therefore . . .' (Luke 10.2, RSV). Where churches pray for the people they need, God seems to answer them.

PREACHING THEM IN

Sermons are a great way to build a church vision and to reinforce it. If people know what the staffing needs are and hear them expounded then they will be on the lookout for those with the right gifts. The Volunteer Centre has produced an excellent booklet about using volunteers, which suggests that team leaders need three qualities to build teams: self-knowledge, self-control and willing submission to authority.[5] These qualities can be taught from the pulpit.

ENCOURAGING THE GIFTING OF THE HOLY SPIRIT

Every church suffers from people volunteering for the wrong jobs. Lay people suffer from their gifts going unrecognized and their talents unused. Matching gifts and posts and encouraging people to seek those gifts that will build up the church is an important part of getting the work done. My own principle has always been as far as possible to encourage people to follow their gifting, even if it has meant leaving posts vacant, and to trust God to fill them, rather than to constrain people to follow my agenda of needs.

PRODUCING A CLEAR BRIEF

'Thanks for agreeing to lead the Pathfinders. Go and talk to Sue, who used to lead them, give it a go, and come back to me if you have any major problems.' With such simple sentences have I ruined people's lives! I have learned the hard way that spending time with people in the initial stages of their taking on new posts is time saved a hundred times over. All of us need clear job descriptions, and proper discussion of the direction that the job should take. Otherwise delegation falls over easily into abdication and the new, enthusiastic volunteer is abused and rapidly disillusioned.

GIVING SUPPORT

Those who take on new ministries require initial and ongoing training, plenty of encouragement and a team to be part of. No one should have to take on a voluntary role without support. Often the diocese or other denominational or national group will provide a network of support outside the church, which can be a lifeline.

ENCOURAGING MODELLING

A useful item to include in most job descriptions is that the new leader should be looking out for assistants who will grow and either take over in a few years' time or start a new part of the expanded work.

FORMING POTENTIAL LEADERS

For a church to function properly it will be a teaching and training institute; that is, a place where Christians learn how to learn.

Every teacher knows that the quickest way to learn is to have to teach. This is why seminaries and theological colleges are only a late invention. The senior clergy knew that if you threw a gifted young man with a degree directly into a local church he would usually learn pretty quickly – he had to. The problem is that most churches deny others than the preachers this quick route to learning. The local church is usually a teaching and training institute – for the benefit of the pastors.

Many para-church organizations such as Scripture Union and the UCCF have learned the teaching and training business better than local churches. When the young David Watson,[6] future vicar of St Michael-le-Belfry in York and gifted evangelist, became a Christian at university he was immediately assigned to another student, the young David Sheppard,[7] future Bishop of Liverpool, who saw him regularly and helped him to grow as a young Christian.

The question was, who was being trained? The answer, plainly, is both. If Watson had been assigned to a chaplain or to the pastor of a local church the teaching might have been more sophisticated, but it is unlikely that it would have been so effective. First, Sheppard would himself have lost an important training opportunity; and second, Watson would have understood that discipling is something done by much older professionals.

Of course some pastors would see this as an abrogation of their responsibility. What if the lay person helping the new Christian teaches some heresy or personal enthusiasm rather than the faith of the Church? It takes many years to form a minister in the doctrines of the faith. Can this be short-circuited? 'Would you let a layman learn to be a brain surgeon just by practising on his friends?' is a common way of expressing the objection. But the analogy is not a helpful one. Being a Christian leader is more akin to being a parent than to being a brain surgeon. Certainly there is potential for damage. But warm human relationships make a better learning environment for adults than the lecture room alone.

I helped for some years while in a previous parish to tutor Readers-in-training. (Readers were for many years the only authorized lay ministers in most Anglican churches in England: they help with preaching and teaching, leading worship, and undertaking pastoral work. Increasingly they are given responsibility in leading a congregation.) The system found it hard to believe that anyone under the age of 45 had enough experience to be a Reader. Also it was determined to keep the academic standards high, so that candidates had to labour away at producing essays. The result was a fairly elderly and theory-burdened bunch of Readers. More exciting is the approach of Sir John Harvey-Jones, sometime Chairman of ICI: 'In my years in industry I have seen the capacity of what are described as "ordinary" people to do very complex tasks and take breath-taking responsibility.'[8]

These days, with the average age of the clergy of most denominations increasing, it is important to look for a whole new generation of young leaders. I like the courage of Alec Dickson, the visionary founder of both Voluntary Service Overseas and Community Service Volunteers. When he first tried to float the idea of VSO he met with much opposition. 'Eighteen-year-olds had nothing to offer but their pimples,' sniffed one critic. But with the help of a letter from the Bishop of Portsmouth to the *Sunday Times* asking for school leavers to work overseas in September 1958 the movement was born.[9]

The task of the ordained minister is not to do all the teaching and training but to supervise, encourage and teach the trainers. It is also to learn from the interaction between trainers and trainees. I have been more encouraged by seeing people's lives change as they begin to disciple others than by almost anything else. And in turn I have been rewarded by the fact that my fellow leaders in church are full of enthusiasm to learn because they have questions arising out of practice.

Another fundamental reason why each church is called to be a teaching and training institute is that a church exists not for itself but for the world in which it is set. The problem with the old model of the shepherd ministering to the sheep in pews is that the congregation easily becomes turned in on itself. 'We are here to be fed,' says the congregation, 'and you are here to feed us.' Without any sense of being pastured for a purpose, the church dies.

Of course not every church member can be used to teach and train others. Some will be unwilling, some unable, and some will lack the opportunity. But whereas the present situation encourages the majority of Christians to think of those who accompany others on their faith journey as being the exceptions, a healthy church will see the majority of its members as potential helpers and leaders.

6
Serving the World on Your Doorstep

There is no Mystery so great as Misery.
Oscar Wilde, *The Happy Prince*

THE GOSPEL AND SOCIETY

Two teenage boys called at the vicarage one summer's day, tired, ragged and dirty. They asked for a cup of tea and some bread and while the kettle boiled they rested on the front grass. When we brought the tea they were already lying on their backs fast asleep, and we saw that their shoes had no soles left. They later told us how they had walked all the way from Derby to Kent, searching in vain for work. We found some shoes for them and they said that it was like walking on air.

No one can read the great nineteenth-century novels of Dickens or Mrs Gaskell without being made freshly aware of the connection between the gospel and the desire for justice in society. No one can read the great socialist novels of the last century such as Upton Sinclair's *The Jungle* (1906), Robert Tressell's *The Ragged Trousered Philanthropist* (1914), or John Steinbeck's *The Grapes of Wrath* (1939), without seeing how laissez-faire capitalism can become godless and evil. In the nineteenth century John Ruskin in his *Unto This Last* (1860) and General Booth in his *In Darkest England and the Way Out* (1890) both laid out (from their rather different perspectives) a Christian critique of social evils and a programme for social reform, which inspired the first Labour members of parliament and served to encourage a systematic approach to pensions, unemployment and poverty.[1] After the Second World War the founding of the welfare state and the

National Health Service produced a consensus on the political left and right, which led to 25 years of growth in social services, health and education.

However, in the second half of the 1970s it became clear that even the moderate socialism of the British Labour Party was not going to solve all the problems of society and there was a radical swing of the pendulum back to the right. Two decades of determined privatization of nationally owned industries, utilities and services followed. Competition and the private market were introduced into the National Health Service, along with managers who had had no medical training. Mental asylums were closed and the patients decanted into the community. Private sponsors were sought in education. The fall of the Berlin Wall in 1989 and the collapse of the Soviet Empire augmented the feeling in the minds of many that socialism had been defeated by capitalism in the titanic battle of the twentieth century.

The results by the turn of the millennium were a rise in general prosperity, particularly in the City of London, a fall in unemployment and inflation, an ever-widening gap between rich and poor, the near collapse of transport, and crises both perceived and real in education and health, law and order, insurance and pensions, immigration and race relations. Manufacturing industry continued its long decline. No one could claim that things are as bad as they had been in nineteenth-century Britain, let alone as bad as in most of Africa and Asia today. Many even claim that to have general prosperity, poverty for an underclass is essential: 'You can't make an omelette without breaking eggs.' But the steady progress which was taken for granted in the 1950s and 1960s has not continued, and we find ourselves in the UK with social services which are noticeably inferior to those of our European neighbours.

All this presents the churches with a twofold gospel challenge. The first is to produce a proper Christian understanding of social relations that could form the foundation for a campaign for changes in law and policy. The second is to work with others in order to produce good local schemes that will meet pressing needs, both locally and more widely. The two can be brought together in the pulpit and housegroups by coherent Bible teaching, discussion and action.

POLITICS AND FAITH

Politics and faith are a potent mixture, and the example of Ulster is enough to convince most people that the two should be kept firmly separate. In British polite society there has long been a shibboleth that religion and politics do not mix. Partly this is temperamental dislike of too much emotion in public life. More importantly it is because all three main political parties have strong church roots. Hence no party can have a monopoly of the Christian vote or an exclusive claim to the word 'Christian' in its title.

Moreover many popular recent readings of the New Testament have tended to address individual consciences rather than communities. This is not difficult, because the early Christian documents were written by a despised minority who had no responsibility for government; but it is possible only if the Old Testament is ignored. In Old Testament times it was clear that all rulers were answerable to God and had a responsibility to rule their people in equity and justice. Both modern unfettered capitalism and modern unfettered socialism are ideologies that fall far short of what God enjoins on his people. It was not only the prophets like Amos who railed at rulers who crush the poor. The whole of salvation history is shot through with the dynamic of a God who rescues his people from slavery, who cares for the widow and the orphan and who commands his people to provide for the poor and the migrant worker.[2]

Once the Old Testament evidence has been noticed it is easy to see that the same themes are far from absent in the New. The parable of Dives and Lazarus shows that when the gap between rich and poor reaches a certain extent, it angers God.[3] The gap between rich and poor in our own world is of this extent. Much more of Jesus' teaching is about the dangerous grip that Mammon, the god of wealth, has on our human hearts than is often noticed in our pulpits. The Pauline epistles analyse social and political structures in terms of powers and principalities opposed to Christ and his Church. Although small and politically powerless, the infant Church took care to model the kind of society in which mutual care and sharing of wealth and goods were the norm.

The twentieth-century bashfulness in our Western churches about the connections between the gospel and social justice has been a kind of capitulation to the secular consensus of our public life. This secular consensus cannot understand the friction between the Islamic Middle East and the Judaeo-Christian West and South, and regularly reduces it to an economic or social debate. But the hatred of Israel by much of the Muslim world is not a secular matter. The dislike and suspicion with which a significant proportion of ordinary people in the 20–20 latitudes of the world regard the USA and Britain is more religious than social. Indeed for the vast majority of the world's population it is not true that religion is an individual or private matter, to be excluded from public policy and debate. Social and political matters cannot be neglected by local churches. If good theology is not being practised then the vacuum will be filled with bad theology and worse politics.

In the UK the Christian faith has for many centuries been 'established' as the bedrock on which all other public values and policies were designed to be based. The word 'establishment' is often carelessly used to denote a privileged position for the Church of England. If 'establishment' means pomp and privilege for one denomination then the Church of England should campaign to disestablish. If, however, it means that the relationship between the basics of faith and the aims of policy is settled ('stable') then we should rise to the challenge.[4] The Christian Church has been given as part of its public duty the vocation to serve the nation by pointing out the connections between policy and values; this is a service we can embrace with enthusiasm as Wilberforce and the Clapham Sect did in their campaigns to reform morals and abolish slavery. The task is to re-educate our people to the implications of these connections, to bring back the vocabulary of the values and the faith commitments behind policies – a vocabulary that has been all but lost. The Jubilee 2000 'Drop the Debt' campaign, which successfully persuaded many industrialized nations to relinquish some of the crippling debts owed to them by developing companies, was largely run by the churches; it shows what can be done.

The relationship between Church and society feels very different in different social contexts. To give an obvious example, a dual-purpose worship centre behind the supermarket on a large outer-urban estate will not have as many baptisms and weddings as a Saxon building at the centre of a market town. A diocese or regional grouping of churches has a particularly valuable part to play in enabling Christians to think biblically about political and social issues. In most parts of England it is possible to travel in half an hour from places where church people (of all denominations) have voted Conservative for generations to equally solid Labour districts where no one with integrity could vote other than socialist. What is needed, and what the churches are uniquely well placed to do, is to bring groups of people together and to enable them to taste one another's social contexts, hear one another's convictions and to let those be tempered by the teaching of Christ.

In Canterbury the Council of Churches has a lively link with churches in Brixton, which has caused many of us to think more deeply about social policy and the economic and social forces that both bind us together and force us apart. Our link sprang, like so many others, from *Faith in the City*, that brave initiative of Robert Runcie, which in 1985 revealed for the first time how much the modern Church was contributing to community-building in the wastelands of neglected UK cities.[5] In the next ten years over £20 million was raised by the churches in support of imaginative projects in urban priority areas, and many brave clergy showed that they were determined not to join the flight from the inner cities. Two decades on, the Church Urban Fund is still distributing millions of pounds annually to new projects in inner cities, and producing signs of hope instead of despair.

In a democracy some of the responsibility that rulers used to bear falls on citizens. For Christians this means a challenge to work and pray for the kind of society that will reflect the character of God and his just and gentle rule. For we will be answerable to him for the kind of government that our votes have encouraged. It also means that we will urge upon our representatives in government their responsibilities towards the poor, the homeless and the hungry, not just in our own country but worldwide. Overseas links and international mission projects bring home to suburban congregations the near slavery that the global market imposes upon many of our brothers and sisters. The proportion of GDP given in aid is scandalously low in comparison with the sums earned by our arms sales.

THE RESPONSIBILITY OF THE LOCAL CHURCH

Real Christianity cannot but share the lives of the poor, the marginal and the destitute. If we have a God who did not think it enough to thunder instructions from Sinai but came to live among us[6] and show us what love is, then the Church too is called not just to talk about love but to show it, in the most practical ways possible.

How a local church does this is something that depends on a complex interaction of local circumstances, its vision and resources, and not least upon the guidance that will come through waiting on God together. But the principles and the mandates to the churches are clear:

- Christians are called to have a worldwide vision and a worldwide responsibility. Issues such as globalization, war and peace, race, environmentalism, debt and world trade demand a worldwide perspective, because 'God so loved the world . . .' Mission, relief and development work will attract our praying, our money and our gifted people. Some churches make a point of sending young leaders for a life-changing trip to a location in the two-thirds world as part of their training.
- We have a responsibility in national and regional politics. It can plainly be an abuse of the pulpit to promote one political party or to produce simplistic solutions to complex social problems, and yet each of our major political parties has an approach to issues of justice and social ethics that cries out for a biblical analysis and response.
- We have a responsibility in local and city/county politics. A well-thought-out project or two can model this responsibility to church members. For instance, in rural Kent there are many business people who live in picture-villages but work in

London and take decisions there that affect the lives of those who live in deprived urban areas of London. Charities and campaigning groups such as Pecan, which has transformed the employment prospects of thousands of out-of-work people in Peckham, have done so in part by making links between commuters and the areas through which they travel.[7]

- We have a responsibility in the local community. It goes without saying that if 'the Lord is here; his Spirit is with us' then his presence will have an impact on those among whom we live and work. To be light and salt, a city (community) that cannot be hid, is part of the first calling of Christian disciples.
- We have a responsibility to the social and financial needs of church members. 'See how those Christians love one another' is only the natural result of the outworking of the gospel.

ON THE DOORSTEP

One of the great pressures upon those living in a vicarage on site is the stream of people who call at the door, expecting practical help. It is not always appreciated by those who manage the welfare state that when the teachers, social workers, benefit advisers, doctors and housing officers leave their offices after a hard week's work on Friday evening, the poor are still with us. The clergy are usually the only professionals who live among the poor, and who live where they work. The trouble is that there are more and more people who are genuinely poor and jobless in a society that is apparently getting richer and richer. On the margins of this poverty are the homeless and asylum seekers. Some of them have discovered that if they play by the rules they will always be excluded, so they might as well bend the rules a bit. For instance, it is not too hard for a homeless alcoholic to obtain sickness benefit – after all he is sick, or will soon make himself so. Benefits are paid out once a fortnight, and if you are an alcoholic and homeless it is frequently too much of a temptation not to drink most of the fortnight's allowance on Thursday night. Then on Friday or Saturday evening, when you are hungry, cold and penniless, you have to start fending for yourself. That is when you call on the local clergy and remind them of Matthew 25.

Clergy grow tough pretty quickly over this kind of behaviour, but are also willing to be duped from time to time in order not to miss the possibility of someone in genuine need going without help. Also, although they may not appear poor, clergy share with those who knock on their doors an experience of what financial hardship can do to people. We want to help; but it is difficult not to get cynical because of all the scams we see.

Just before we left Folkestone a van pulled up outside the parsonage and a grey-faced middle-aged man knocked on the door. 'It's the wife; she's an invalid and she's on oxygen in the back. I've got to get her home to Plymouth and I've run out of petrol. Can you help us out?' I duly inspected the wife who was indeed lying in the back of the van breathing heavily through a mask. It was a Saturday night and it seemed churlish to doubt the story – so I produced the money. Then we moved to Canterbury, and a month or two later the same van drew up at the door. The driver did not remember me, but I certainly remembered him!

Shortly afterwards someone appeared who said he had just been beaten up and had been treated in hospital. Could I help him out? Something was not quite right about this figure: he was rather too dramatically swathed in bandages; so I followed him up the garden path. By the gate was a taxi with two friends in it, already quite merry and puffing at cigars, eagerly waiting for the money I would provide via his ruse for their Saturday night out!

What to do about the most blatant fraudsters? The local clergy here have developed an informal hotline so that we can warn colleagues about those who go from presbytery to manse collecting funds with false stories and about those who might be violent. Church offices, often manned by part-time or voluntary workers also need a procedure to deal with some of the more alarming characters who turn up at reception.[8]

Usually the harm has not been great from these scams, but there have been some extremely unpleasant experiences. And I have lost count of the number of family and social events that have been disrupted by drunk and incapable people refusing to go away.

I learned years ago that it is not much use talking to a drunk – he won't take it in and he won't remember a word when he sobers up, but that doesn't mean you can just get rid of someone. We had a supper party one evening and a particularly voluble man arrived. He had gone into church, found the choir practising and the organist had sent him to the vicarage. He was glad to find people and food and, with several front teeth missing, cheerfully monopolized the discussion. As they had come from a wealthy London church and he had just finished a prison sentence for credit card fraud, there were several amusing moments.

In fact it has not by any means all been bad. One evening I was summoned to a room where a women's group was about to meet. They had found in the darkened room a large and desperate man whose face was covered with blood and his clothes with vomit. We discovered under the filth a charming person who as a result of long-standing family problems had turned to drink and was quite near to death. We cleaned him up and gave him a bed. Jane put his clothing through three wash-cycles; to her chagrin his rather expensive Norwegian sweater shrank to a child's size. The house stank for days and we had to burn the bedding. He became a friend, found a good job as a gardener locally and sometimes even came to church. Eventually he told us how he had been to the King's School, Canterbury, and how his father's over-high expectations of him had caused a breakdown.

Dave entered our lives as we unpacked the removal van. He needed money so I asked him to paint our bookshelves. For the next 14 years I looked at the crazy streaks he had bequeathed to us and wished I had simply given him the money! He came back to us periodically because he had fathered a child locally and would try to make a home with the mother. When he was sober he was friendly and helpful, but when he was drunk he was maudlin and impossible. It was all too easy for him to pull a bottle of spirits off the tempting displays in the supermarkets, hide it under his jacket, and leave, paying only for a loaf of bread or some cigarettes. Once he tried less successfully to hide a video recorder under his jacket and was absent for several months as Her Majesty's guest. One Christmas midnight he arrived at the service very drunk and Jane stayed with him at the back of church while he poured out his life story to her; Christmas is the very worst time of year for people without friends or family. He was singing 'Take time to be holy', and revealed that one of the sources of his distress was that his mother had always prayed for him and he had let her down so badly. A week or so later he came back to church, sober this time, asking for prayer. Jane and some others took him aside. As she prayed over him and the wreckage of his life, Dave grew more and more astonished that she knew so much about him; he of course did not remember all that he had told her on Christmas Eve. 'How did you know that about me? You have the gift of prophecy!' he exclaimed. When we finally left Canterbury and the streaky bookshelves had been loaded into the removal van, Dave came to wave us off. 'Hi, babe!' he said to Jane. 'We go back a long way!' It certainly felt so.

One day we were entertaining some guests to lunch. Among them was an agnostic reader in social policy from the university. After a couple of the usual callers had knocked at the door and we had answered questions from our surprised guests about them, the professor could not help saying that, whereas she taught about social action on behalf of the excluded, we were living it. It was an unexpected compliment.

SINFUL STRUCTURES

After the creation of the welfare state there seemed, for a generation at least, to be less and less for voluntary groups to do. The main social problems had not disappeared, but were being systematically worked at by government agencies. But in the last two decades of the twentieth century the churches woke up to the fact that social problems were increasing again. For instance, in the 1960s and 1970s beggars and homeless people were a rarity. In the 1980s they started to appear again and since the 1990s they are everywhere. The numbers of jobless increased to over three million. Was the phrase 'Victorian values' a sign that we were returning to Disraeli's two nations and the social conditions that inspired the Salvation Army?

All the churches in our area agreed that something needed to be done about the changes in society and the public policy which had resulted in this flood tide of misery on our streets. Most denominations soon agreed that that we could not stay out of it and we should as much as possible act together and create a climate of opinion in which homelessness, extreme poverty and mass unemployment would be seen as unacceptable.

For many years there had been a monthly clergy, voluntary workers and social services lunch in Canterbury and this provided contacts with those who knew what was happening in the housing market and what could be usefully contributed by the voluntary sector. Sometimes these people from housing and social services, who had spent years of their working lives trying to be of service to the poor in the area, would almost break down as they described how their work was being destroyed by new legislation and reduction in funding. Sometimes we clergy felt near to tears too. Everywhere there appeared new structural weaknesses in the fabric of the welfare state.

One of the most obvious problems was the lack of direct-access housing anywhere in the area. Someone arriving at the major ports of Dover or Folkestone without accommodation, or someone thrown out of home anywhere in the Canterbury area had nowhere to turn to. The nearest hostel for the homeless was miles away at Sittingbourne and, now that travel warrants were no longer available from the police, it might as well be on the moon. One of the clergy and several lay people joined the new housing forum, which at once set up a lodgings register with the Citizens' Advice Bureau and tried to find ways of making more cheap rented accommodation available. We lobbied the local MP and councillors and we supported the new housing associations and especially the Cyrenians, who from small beginnings managed to produce a significant amount of housing.

The government and city council were not idle either and started to make more money available to those treating alcohol-related problems. Our own parish found itself with many institutions planned to ease the intolerable pressures: an excellent unattached youth project, a hostel for homeless teenagers, a centre for treating alcoholics; all of them with funding from the state. We kept pushing, praying, giving and lobbying. And then the housing minister, to our surprise, announced that government money would be available to fund a direct-access unit for the city, so that at last single homeless people would be able to apply for a bed for the night and be given an opportunity to sort out their lives.

This was wonderful news, but the question was, What to do until then? You could hardly ask a homeless person to wait two years for a bed! The churches decided to act together immediately and devised a three-level response. The first was the continuation of the build-up of private initiatives by each church, taking in those we judged safe to have in the house, finding basements and garages for others; the Pentecostal minister produced survival bags and so it went on. The second was the soup run, an initiative managed by Christians Together in Canterbury. Seven nights a week, manned by volunteers from different churches, this provides soup and sandwiches in the city centre for anything up to 50 people a night between 9 and 10 p.m. It is a heroic ministry and I am full of admiration for the men and women, often elderly, who come with their thermos flasks and set up their stall in all weathers, dealing cheerfully and courageously with whoever approaches them, including sometimes the abusive and raging drunk. Life is not much fun out on the streets and some of the young who have left home or been kicked out have been brought up in a culture without pity.

The third initiative was the voucher scheme. We wanted to provide overnight accommodation for those who appeared on our doorsteps, but we knew it was not safe to take most of them into our homes. We set up a fund, paid for and administered by the churches, to give emergency overnight accommodation at a bed-and-breakfast establishment. The scheme works in the following way. If a homeless person calls on a minister who believes it right to help him (usually it is him), the minister takes him down to the police station and the police note his name and check his identity and then give him a voucher. The minister then escorts him to the landlady who, if the person is reasonably sober, takes him in and sends in the voucher with the bill to the treasurer. The police have been enthusiastic with their help and have provided useful objectivity: they prevent people going from minister to minister each night asking for more help, and they can spot someone who has been let out of prison with an accommodation allowance which he wants to drink. The money that the churches have provided for this scheme is not enough to end homelessness in Canterbury. But it has provided emergency housing for many different people from all over the country who have been stranded without a bed for the night. It has also been a way in which those clergy and families, who by living on site are particularly exposed to knocks on the door late at night, can do something practical to help.

Is homelessness a temporary phenomenon which can be alleviated through the government's initiative on rough sleepers or, as many fear, a permanent structural feature of our society, one of the results of the collapse of marriage and the family unit? This most grave of social problems shows that there is need for churches, particularly if they work ecumenically, to make a difference politically and socially at local level. To call it 'ambulance work' is unfair and inaccurate. Some of the schemes that the churches have devised to meet the needs of asylum seekers are models we can be extremely proud of. In a social democracy we are able to influence decision-making as well as to help people.

The churches are in a unique position to mediate over other structural problems in the welfare state. The policy of closing large mental hospitals and entrusting people to 'Care in the Community' has had great benefits but has also resulted in large numbers of inadequate people in sore need of care and attention being left to fend for themselves. Sometimes we try to give them jobs to enable them to earn some food or pocket money, but it is not easy to find appropriate tasks when by definition they need professional help. I was particularly sad last summer when one lad with a twitch and a speech impediment who kept calling on us and whom we tried unsuccessfully to help was found face down in a lake nearby. His drug regime had not been monitored closely enough.

Another time we found a homeless woman called Hilda sleeping in the churchyard. She had been on the road for years and was reaching that stage in life where she was no longer strong enough to survive the Kentish winters. We discovered that without an address a homeless person cannot start on the housing ladder. So we took her in. You soon find that you cannot patronise the poor:

Hilda would not sleep in the sheets we gave her because they were poly-cotton and she would only have natural fibres next to her. However, she stayed for a few weeks and was able to use our address as her own to get a council flat. She had a tremor but was full of fun and used to come to services and shake at the back. Members of our church gave her meals and invited her round. I took her funeral eventually, but it was not a sad occasion.

But forming local opinion is not without its dangers. The local press takes a keen interest in what the churches are doing so that if there is any whiff of dispute it can be blown up into a headline. Some experiences will stay with me for life. When the miners' strike was at its height and the pit villages of Kent were being devastated by the closing of their mines, our church was reported widely and accurately as being sympathetic to the villagers who were losing their industry and their livelihood. As many of the miners were the grandchildren of Durham miners who had lived through the Great Depression of the 1920s and had moved to Kent to find work, the sense of being abandoned by comfortable Britain was intense and bitter. We petitioned Parliament on the subject. Through a careless headline or two, the miners of one village received the (quite false) idea that our church was the only one in the area that was publicly defending them against the government, and this led to all sorts of misunderstanding. One amusing side effect among all the tragedy came a couple of years later. A Conservative councillor approached us to say that can-vassers from her party would not be calling at our house in future because we had helped the miners and were clearly 'a lost cause'!

LEADERSHIP CAN MAKE A DIFFERENCE

Clergy understand the dynamics of community ministry and the strengths and weaknesses of congregations. We have all experienced the little cliques in village churches who keep the church going and keep the village from the church. Or the mobile cliques in a suburban area who come from well outside the parish and decide what the people living in the parish 'really' need for their welfare. Because the gap between 'haves' and 'have nots' is not as stark in Britain as in, say, South America, the insights of liberation theology have not generally been seen as applicable here. On the contrary it is all too easy for clergy, who necessarily try to inculturate their gospel, to become part of the social structure, part of the 'establishment' in precisely the wrong sense. That is not a gospel role for a minister. Being seen and known around the parish is an important preliminary to making a difference, but it is not the same thing. Clergy often speak of the need to turn up at community events to 'fly the flag' or to 'loiter with intent' but both phrases have a tendency to become empty metaphors.

If we are to promote a renewed kingdom community, which will obey the Scripture by not being conformed to this world but transformed, then a strategy is necessary. To provide pastoral care is important but not enough. The powers need confronting, the comfortable need challenging, and the love in the community needs releasing. All this is a work of the Spirit.

A few years ago a working party helped our church to undertake a survey, to see how many unemployed, sick and elderly there were in the parish and, even more important, to ask people what they perceived the needs of the community to be. We discovered many needs we could pray about and act upon, and that many more people than we had expected were articulating deeply felt spiritual needs. Our feeble attempts to come out of our church building to understand what it felt like to be them met with a warm response. It was as if they were looking for their local church to take a lead, and that our willingness to help in practical ways could enable them to open up about their spiritual needs. This simple survey provided us with the foundation for a strategy and ideas that led into action for many years.

After the initial strategy the next stage (according to liberation theology) is what the French call *révision de vie*. When a church engages successfully with its community it sets up group work with the unemployed or other disadvantaged groups and does Bible study, which enables them to connect their inner and outer lives. The result is that suddenly the group discovers that categories like 'salvation' and 'righteousness', which had previously seemed to them like religious jargon for the in-group, spring to life as powerful connectors to the love of God for their daily life and work. Life changes. I have been to fascinating events with our

French link diocese in which we heard moving accounts of how unchurched groups of young workers had discovered the power of Bible study and felt empowered by the love of Christ for them.

I wish I could say that our church was as successful in 'empowering the poor' as this but – though several unchurched individuals and couples certainly do discover a whole new way of looking at their lives in the light of Scripture and are empowered to start a new life, and though our church does wrestle with its community involvement – we remain on the whole firmly part of comfortable Britain. Often we have the sense that people from the parish come to our services – drawn perhaps by the vitality of the worship or the enthusiastic commendation of members – bringing great inner burdens or sadnesses and leave afterwards with the same burdens. An outwardly 'successful' church can easily give the impression that God is not for the unsuccessful, the depressed, the lonely, the poor and the unemployed.

Nevertheless the joy of being rooted in a local community is that we are able to make important differences to people's lives. Debt is one of the large hidden problems of our society. Loan sharks are some of the biggest users of the mail service. One of our wardens is a probation officer and experienced debt counsellor. From time to time she has sat down with a family from our church who have been seduced into high levels of debt by unscrupulous credit card operators, has solemnly cut up all their cards, and enabled them (often with the help of a cash injection from the church) to start new financial disciplines, which have freed them from debt over the coming months. Someone on very low wages was helped by some well-qualified professionals in the congregation to set up his own business and to keep more of the money he earned. A young couple lost their main source of income and were in danger of losing their home. Their housegroup leaders gave them a substantial gift to keep their mortgage payments going. Later, when the young couple moved away with their work, they sent a large cheque to vicar and wardens for the establishment of a 'church family fund' to enable the church to support individuals at times of crisis. Many are helped by this fund, and many pay into it.

What should not be forgotten, however, is the achievement of many urban, suburban and rural churches in our generation. Our parish is rightly proud of the fact that Age Concern in our city was started by a member of our church 30 years ago and has maintained Age Concern lunches in our church hall every week since then, with an army of volunteers and two or three gifted and determined leaders. I know of several churches where detached and attached youth workers have made a real impact on the local drug scene and have enabled generations of young people to discover faith in God and in themselves. Together the churches of Canterbury have for many years supported a pregnancy counselling service and a hostel so that girls who become pregnant by mistake can discuss all the options before making decisions about the baby. Most local churches have similar stories to be proud of. What is needed is the determination to meet the challenges of today with a similarly large vision.

It is the task of the ordained ministry along with lay colleagues to discern how best to give public expression to the concerns of those who do not have a voice in the community, to have a church vision that embodies the promise of Jesus that 'the meek shall inherit the earth' and to ensure that the pastoral work of the parish amounts to more than comforting the already comfortable.

The example of David Sheppard, Michael Eastman and many others has given much assistance to churches in enabling them to have a proper, gospel 'bias to the poor'.[9] But it is the work of Christians in the two-thirds world that speaks most clearly with the voice of the Lord.[10] The challenge to the churches of the West is how to translate that voice into our own very different political and social context. It is Ann Morisy who has perhaps attempted this most successfully in her helpful book, *Beyond the Good Samaritan*.[11]

COMMUNITIES OF RECONCILIATION

On 12 February 1993 a toddler called James Bulger was picked up by a couple of ten-year-old lads in a Liverpool shopping centre and heartlessly killed. The nation was shocked that juveniles could show such cruelty. The Home Secretary changed the law to enable him to have the young men imprisoned for 15 years. In 2001 there was a successful appeal to the European Court in Strasbourg to have the sentences reduced. There was a widespread public debate about justice and mercy, the existence of evil and the difference between revenge and punishment. Germaine Greer, feminist, agnostic and professor of English literature at Warwick University, said on an *Any Questions?* programme on BBC Radio 4 that what was needed was communities who would not only welcome Jon Venables and Robert Thompson, the young offenders, into their midst after their time in gaol, but who would publicly commit themselves to helping them to start a new life. The two had had tragic childhoods, never knowing the love of a father and so, she said, needed to have love and regular discipline. Not only this, but the community would in effect stand bail for the pair, saying to them that they would take the responsibility if they ever re-offended. This was a challenging pronouncement, reminiscent of Dostoevsky or George Eliot, showing more gospel courage than many a church commentary on the Bulger affair. The idea of the local church acting not only as community of reconciliation but as scapegoat and substitute is stretching and inspiring.

In practice it is demanding. I know of a parish where a respected lay leader was suddenly accused of an isolated act of child abuse some 20 years previously and was given a prison sentence. When he emerged after some months away he supposed that he had paid his debt to society and could resume his church membership and ministry. The vicar had to tell him that though many people in the congregation agreed with him that a simple line could now be drawn under the past, more said that they would walk out of church if he were to reappear. To bring the two sides together would need some intensive teaching and reflection on community forgiveness; perhaps also it would be necessary for the man to speak candidly about his sin and to ask his fellow Christians for their forgiveness and for their help in his healing. Being a community of redemption is a tough calling, but infinitely worthwhile. It can only be worked out in practice; a practice, however, soaked in the New Testament.[12]

A local church can be a liberating body, a model of God's love in action, active in society on behalf of the voiceless. Equally it can be a stifling organization, trapped in easy prejudice, excluding all but the comfortable. That balance – of seeing ourselves as 'work in progress' still needing God's power to change us but not being paralysed thereby – is not easy to achieve. To return to the conclusion of *Faith in the City*:

> We know that there is a transforming power present in human affairs which can resolve apparently intractable situations and can bring new life into the darkest places. If, as we dare to affirm, the true nature of human life is to be discerned in the life of Jesus Christ, we can take heart and pledge ourselves to a deeper commitment to create a society in which benefits and burdens are shared in a more equitable way.[13]

The Bulger affair put an end to what easy optimism was left in our society about a human nature without evil, which could be structured into goodness by appropriate social work and legislation. Only God can redeem. But he chooses to use quite ordinary communities both as samples of work in progress and as instruments for transforming society. There is no body better suited to be an instrument of transformation than the local church.

7
Mission and Evangelism

Evangelism cannot be a program strategy, but [is] a revolutionary way of enacting the hope and energy of the believing community.

Walter Brueggemann[1]

DEFINITIONS

'Mission' and 'evangelism' clearly belong together but have become loaded words, with multiple different shades of meaning for different kinds of Christian. For simplicity, the word 'mission' is used here mainly in its large sense: meaning the whole commissioning and sending work of God. The Father sent his Son into the world to redeem it and together the Father and the Son sent the Holy Spirit to sanctify it. Hence the Church is part of God's mission. It is apostolic, not only in the sense of being in continuity with the teaching and fellowship of the apostles but also in the sense of having been com-missioned, or 'sent'. Mission is not what the Church decides to do, so much as what it is caught up in as a result of what God has decided to do.

The word 'evangelism' is used here to mean the declaring of the evangel, the good news, in order that people may become disciples of Jesus Christ. 'Evangelism' is therefore a more focused word with a narrower coverage than 'mission'. To take a simple example, encouraging church members to volunteer as part-time drivers for Age Concern could count as part of the church's 'mission' but probably not of its 'evangelism'.

MISSION AS THE PRESENCE OF JESUS

Whereas John the Baptist, like the Old Testament prophets, was called to be a herald of the good news of the coming of the kingdom, Jesus both proclaimed the good news and embodied it. He was the evangel. By the Spirit he still does proclaim and still is the good news through his body, the Church.

Once, as we moved into a new parish and were still unpacking, a Free Church minister arrived on our doorstep to greet us and invite us to help lead a city-wide evangelistic campaign. Our church wardens had been praying for more evangelism in the parish for some time and encouraged me to become co-chairman of the organizing committee. The Roman Catholics, the Free Churches and we ourselves worked and prayed for two years towards the campaign, and when the week came we all but filled the cathedral nave for several nights. It was an exciting time and much ecumenical progress was made but afterwards, as we followed up those who had responded, we realized that, though other churches had received converts, not a single adult had been added to our church. What had happened to all the prayer and hard work? Strangely, a year later, we noticed that our church had grown full on Sunday mornings. There were many new Christians. What was God saying to us?

In the latter part of the twentieth century there was considerable polarization about mission and evangelism. There were churches that longed to have evangelistic programmes, but there were many others who believed that such campaigns were an embarrassment, that the presence of the Church was to be the good news, and the campaigns for peace and justice were to be its evangelism.

There were also still corners of the Anglican Church with a pastoral and static view of the world. England is basically Christian (said this view), and the calling of the Church, especially in the persons of its ministers, is to be chaplain to the nation, to visit and comfort and give spiritual support at all levels of society. Mission that involved campaigns or 'targeting' people-groups with the gospel was at best an intrusion and at worst a denial of God's love. In Kent we met on more than one occasion in the course of our visiting the assertion that mission was not necessary here because they had already had a mission in 597. People had clearly done a primary school project on Augustine, which had successfully inoculated them against the gospel!

During the 1990s the Decade of Evangelism brought about a sea change in the debate. More and more parishes came to realize that the position of the church is quite different from the pastoral chaplaincy model. We live not in a static but in a fast-changing, largely post-Christian and neo-pagan world. Fresh study of the New Testament convinced many advocates of so-called presence evangelism that the promise of the continuing presence of Jesus in the Church is connected with our engagement in mission.[2] In John's Gospel, Jesus commands his apostles to abide in his love and so to bear fruit for the kingdom by going out in mission. In Matthew's Gospel he promises to be with them as they go and make disciples.[3] Not the least of the achievements of the Decade of Evangelism has been to make evangelism part of church life again for the average parish. Equally, those parishes that majored on proclamation evangelism have come to see that proclamation without incarnation can become little more than a sales patter. It ignores both our nuanced spiritual history and the fact that the gospel is more than words.

In some ways it is refreshing and bracing to compare ourselves to the first Christian generations before the time of Constantine. Like them we can unashamedly announce the good news. But our situation is more complex than theirs. We are surrounded in our culture with monuments to past faith. Our institutions in government, health and education still have largely Christian foundations and principles, which should not be lightly abandoned.[4] Our church schools and colleges are worth fighting for. Our literature and cultural history cannot be understood except as a dialogue with the gospel. When there is a church building on almost every corner of the land we cannot pretend that no one has ever heard the gospel before, ignorant though most people may now be of its content.

In the mid-1990s different denominations combined to support a number of evangelistic efforts to 'reach the nation for Christ' by posters and literature. For instance an initiative of the Pentecostal Church called JIM (Jesus in Me) sought to provide opportunities for local churches based on a high-profile national advertising campaign. The organizers pronounced it a 'qualified success' but the fact remains that this kind of evangelism ignores the reality that hardly any one in the West lives out of reach of a church and of Christians. People may not have encountered Jesus Christ themselves or had close contact with those who have a living relationship with him. But will a poster campaign change that? More seriously, if people do believe us and join us, will they find the churches live up to the claims? The public perception is that our culture has grown out of a restrictive and belligerent religious past as we have grown out of believing in fairies and a flat earth. How can the Church proclaim and be good news to our world?

The place to start is at the other end, with God and his great mission of love in Christ Jesus. The biblical model for the good news is that the Egyptian and Babylonian captivities were a type of the deeper human captivity of sin and death.[5] What is the good news for our generation? At bottom it must be for ever the same, the love of God for everything he has made, centred on the cross of Christ and his defeat of sin and death. But above the foundation it is context-sensitive. We can see this from the encounters of Jesus with his contemporaries or from the epistles and journeys of Paul or from the letters of John to the seven churches of Asia. Jesus did not appear to have a system that he offered indiscriminately to those he encountered. Nor did the apostles, though a rich theology of their mission can be worked out by studying their writings and journeys. It is not the way of love to package salvation. Love goes to spend itself.

REACHING OUT IN THE THIRD MILLENNIUM

Our generation has lost the sense of private sin that characterized the later Christian centuries and has instead rediscovered a more primitive sense of public shame (notably in the case of paedophiles). Significantly there has been a disappearance of public hope.[6] Cynicism is the shared faith of our time. The breakdown of family and community, the rise in youth crime and violence have contributed to a profound alienation in the most prosperous democracies in history. The individual is prized and courted not for his or her intrinsic worth but as a consumer; as producer he or she can be discarded at the whim of the global market. The absurd sexualization of our culture is a frenetic attempt to deny the existence of death and decay. Much public humour has a function in our society of easing and disguising the wound produced by the fact that the promises of happiness, wealth and eternal youth, so freely given by advertising and politicians, cannot be delivered.

Contemporary novels are full of the disjunctions produced by such a society. One sharp, sad, and funny example of such a commentary is *The Lawnmower Celebrity*.[7] A father and his teenage son are at loggerheads, with hilarious results. The son survives only a few days in any job before chaos descends and he is sacked. Only gradually does it become heartbreakingly clear that the reason why the father and son are unable to relate, or to behave normally, is because the wife and mother has been dying of cancer, and they have no means of dealing with this. The strange behaviour that provides the humour is a kind of addictive and compulsive diversionary activity.

To a society that is trapped in compulsive diversionary activity, the Holy Spirit brings the good news of reconciliation, forgiveness, meaning – and life that is able to face death. The plan is to do it in and through the Church, through us who are both victors and captives in the triumphal procession of Christ.[8] But we can only do this if we are ourselves being evangelized. In the Roman Mass the priest cannot give the bread of life to the people before he has himself taken it, saying, 'Lord, I am not worthy to receive you, but only say the word and I shall be healed.'[9] Equally a local church cannot bring good news to its parish except in so far as it can point to itself as a community being healed.

Where in a local church there are the comparatively rare but real instances of miracles, or the more common but equally wonderful changes in relationships and characters, then there is good news, which will spread quickly. People tell their friends. Where the church is being itself, i.e. part of God's mission, then it will be naturally an attractive force for good in the community. Neighbours are curious and come to see what is happening. Because the Age of the Spirit is the Age of the Church, the Church is part of the good news it proclaims. The life of the local church is lived out in two dimensions: we both share in the frustrations and pain of the fallen world we inhabit, and we also already taste the future when Christ will reign over all the nations and God's forgiving love will finally transform us completely.

In church growth literature it is rightly pointed out that where the Church is being the Church, spiritual growth will be normal, and spiritual growth will normally lead to numerical growth.[10] Growth does not need to be engineered. As John Wimber used to say, 'Healthy sheep reproduce.' It takes an abnormal situation for sheep to stop breeding, for love to stop reproducing. Where the love of Christ is, there will be a natural spreading of the good news, in word and deed.

Looking back on our 'failed' city evangelistic campaign with the benefit of hindsight, it is clear that 'failure' was too hasty a judgement. In taking part in a mission exercise the Christians of our town were receiving training in how the gospel works, and clarifying in our own hearts and minds what the content of the gospel is. We were also leaving behind some prejudices about neighbouring congregations of different denominations. One concrete result of the joint endeavour was that we continued to hold lively monthly ecumenical celebrations for several years afterwards. The apparently artificial exercise of mounting a series of events revealed all sorts of strengths which could be celebrated and weaknesses which could be attended to; we were in effect asking the Spirit to evangelize us. It was little wonder, then, that as visitors visited our church, they noticed that God was a little more visibly at work, and we were better able to welcome them, and more equipped to lead them into a saving relationship with their Lord. When we opened ourselves more to God's good news, he sent more people.

So the Decade of Evangelism not only succeeded in putting evangelism back at the centre of church life, but also turned some of the vicious cycles of decline into virtuous cycles of health. In the Church of England the Archbishops of Canterbury and York took several initiatives, which quietly equipped the Church for action and provided a platform for future growth in a hostile climate. The establishment of 'Springboard' as a travelling group of gifted people who would train parishes and dioceses in appropriate evangelism and model different ways of relevant proclamation has been widely welcomed. The work of Canon Robert Warren as the Church of England's National Officer for the Decade has enabled many churches to understand what it might mean to become missionary congregations.[11] The working party set up by the archbishops under the chairmanship of Bishop John Finney produced the report *Good News People*, which encourages the nourishing of evangelists at diocesan level. The same working party led to the founding of the national College of Evangelists, which allows people who are engaged in the work of evangelism at national and regional level to have some official support and to be recognized by the archbishops.[12]

Some churches have lost the social momentum to make an impact on their parish. However, where things have become so low that a church is near to closing it can liberate its leaders to try some radical missionary approach. Many a church has found that the decline in numbers has been the opportunity it needed to make changes, and has started to grow again. In some important ways we are better equipped, leaner and fitter than 50 years ago. We certainly understand more about how God creates Christian community and about how such a community is like water to a thirsty ground.

IS OUR CHURCH 'GOOD NEWS'?

The most evangelistic things we do are in fact those things that are basic to community-building, which enable our church family to be and proclaim good news – so basic that they hardly come under the usual definitions of evangelism. You cannot sensibly invite baptism couples to come back to church, for instance, if there is no crèche. Then there is the question of accessibility. People often tell amazing stories of going to churches for weeks at a time – and no one speaks to them. The way that the stewards welcome visitors is often far more important than what the clergy do or say. I sometimes visit churches where I cannot find the way in! I walk from the street round three sides of a large building, trying each closed door I come to, until the forbidding closed door on the fourth side yields to an unlit porch like a Victorian prison. Or a notice-board by the main gate is blank, or tells me that service times vary with the phases of the moon. Ways of obviating these points are of course the basics of being a good news community, but they need revisiting regularly, perhaps with the help of a booklet such as *How Friendly to Strangers is Your Church?*[13]

A healthy local church will also have ways of helping people to come to faith, through appropriate courses and services that are particularly geared to the newcomer and to enquirers, to baptism, wedding and funeral families. For a church to be a proper church there will be mission exercises, to strengthen the evangelistic muscles of the church members and enable them to have the joy of leading their friends and neighbours into a living relationship with God. In a sense the more downbeat, utilitarian and prosaic the systems (confirmation classes with lay helpers, special Mothering Sunday and harvest services, parenting courses, children's holiday clubs and so on) the easier it will be to invite people successfully without them feeling artificially 'targeted'.

The key to leading congregations into mission is to wait upon God together for imaginative ideas that spring naturally from the local context. As a friend of mine often remarks, it is worth invent-ing the wheel again together, because people then own the plans that they have helped to make. What will work well in one locality and at one time depends very much on the guidance of the Spirit and creative imaginations. I think of the case where a woman who was going to start a new all-age service volunteered to become the village lollipop lady, helping the parents and children to cross the busy road outside the school. It was a wonderful way of serving the village and getting to know the children. Families flocked to the new service and many found faith. But it would not work everywhere.

One church takes part in the village pantomime and the result of the church throwing itself enthusiastically into a village enterprise is always new members in church. Parents are always grateful to churches that put on bonfire parties and other safe events where they can bring children and where the generations can mix. Church picnics, outings and walks help to make the friendships and family life more natural. Because the reasons that people do not come to church are usually more cultural than intellectual, social events help people to meet church members on a level where they can see if they are crazy or if there is something real about their faith. A father came to faith recently because he wanted to check up on his daughter who was taking what he felt to be an unhealthy interest in the church; it was helpful to be able to invite him first to a party. We have morris men, Burns Night celebrations, barbecues (invariably in the rain), bank holiday walks, and whatever other events people wish to organize. In his helpful book on evangelism,[14] John Clarke reports on a survey from Essex which indicated that

1 if a friend or relative will come to three *quality* social events in a row, they will start coming to church;
2 if they come to church for three months, they will be willing to join an enquirers' group;
3 of those who join an enquirers' group, a very high percentage become Christians and continue in the faith.

If we are to welcome whole people-groups into our churches then we have to take account of their needs and to go to where they are, both physically and socially. This can sound as if it is pandering to a consumer mentality, but in fact it is seeking to serve the needs of the community; there is a subtle but important distinction. Love will out, and sacrificial love in particular. In a congregation where love is doing its work properly there will be no yawning gap between selfless meeting of the community's practical needs, and the unselfconscious sharing with others of the identity and source of that love. Working at finding the means will all be part of the mission of the church. And it is fun.

Perhaps a word about networking is in order. There is a common prejudice in Church of England circles in favour of 'communal' as opposed to 'associational' church life.[15] According to this thesis a communal church is one where everyone comes from the neighbourhood, where boundaries between churched and unchurched are blurred, where faith is more instinctive than articulated, and leadership and worship are traditional. An associational church, by contrast, is one where the members are committed, articulate, know what they believe, have clear boundaries, travel to church from a wide area and expect relevant worship and to share in leadership. It is obvious that churches differ in these matters and the distinction is at first sight seductive; but in the end largely unhelpful. Very many apparently communal churches are found on closer examination to draw their worshippers from a wide area. People do travel to the church of their choice, for good reasons and bad. More fundamentally, community in our culture is for most people no longer expressed solely in geographical terms. Natural friendships and ties have to do with work, education, leisure, age group, interests and a host of other factors. It is good that local churches (and not just Anglican ones) have a feel for their neighbourhoods. It roots their mission in a concrete social context; and locality is still important, as any estate agent will testify. But if the Church is to evangelize our society afresh it will also want to take account of special interest groups and networks that do not work geographically.

I used to feel guilty when a child from my church invited another child from school to our youth club. The educational catchment area was so arranged that the invited child might live 20 miles away. When in due course the child was confirmed and the vicar rang to complain that the family had started to travel 20 miles from his parish to my church I felt even more guilty. I used to try to refuse to have such children come to my church and tell the family to approach their own parish. The result was, because there was no youth club in that church and because there was no personal contact, that the family did not go anywhere and the child was not confirmed. Here was a child in my youth group evangelizing her peers in a natural way, using the social and educational networks she inhabited, and here was I, putting stumbling blocks in the way because of an outmoded parochialism. Today I would still inform my colleagues, but would not put pressure on new Christians to return to their own parishes until they are strong enough and until there is the possibility of a natural link. It is a joy when one can send back two or three families with a vision for their local church rather than an unsupported individual.

One happy way to keep in touch with people-groups by using the locality is parish visiting. Each summer our custom has been to hold a short training session to which the whole parochial church council and other volunteers are invited. The training emphasizes both the pastoral and the evangelistic opportunities in visiting people in their homes. Then for two or three evenings we divide up part of the parish into convenient roads and go out in twos. Sometimes another group has stayed behind to pray. Invariably people go out nervous but come back rejoicing. They go with a free parish magazine, plus introductory material about the faith. It is interesting how often people welcome a visit from their parish church; how surprised they are that we are not asking for money or selling anything. The direct gains from such a campaign are modest. Most people are too busy to engage in deep conversation with strangers. But the indirect gains are great. It gives church members a focus for their prayers and a greater understanding of how people live in different neighbourhoods. It reinforces contacts and informs people about their local church; very often when I do baptism or bereavement visiting they will pull out a prayer leaflet from behind the clock on the mantelpiece and say, 'Oh, yes, someone from your church called last summer.' It all helps to make the boundaries between church and community pervious, and to enable people to see the church as caring for them, as believing in coming to where they are.

Earlier I said that encouraging church members to volunteer as part-time drivers for Age Concern counted as part of 'mission' rather than 'evangelism', but that in the end is to draw the distinctions too tightly. Where a church is accustomed to welcoming newcomers into the family of Christ, and has a strategy in place for nurturing faith and bringing people to new birth, then all its activity will be coloured by the transforming power of the gospel.

CHURCH PLANTING

As towns expand, church buildings are often marooned at one corner of their parishes. St Mary Bredin in Canterbury, for instance, is a mile away from the population centre at Wincheap. That is no distance in the country, but quite a considerable one in a city. Every day as I walked down to Wincheap County Primary and chatted outside the school gates, waiting to pick up our children, it seemed few parents even knew where St Mary's was.

When the parish church grew overfull in the mid-1980s, we began to discuss the possibility of two projects: first an extension to the church building, and second another Sunday morning service between the 8 a.m. and the 11 a.m. Then the idea came: wouldn't it be more exciting to take the church to the people rather than persuade the people to come to the church? Gradually the thought took root that we might start a new congregation in Wincheap School.

There were the obvious objections. Those worshippers who lived in Wincheap and had always made the effort to come up to the church didn't see why it should be a problem for others to do so. Why worship in a scruffy school hall when you have a fine parish church? What about all the books and furnishings? What about the expense of hiring public premises for a few hours a week? So we settled down in the PCC to pray, and started consulting those who were interested in the project: the bishop, the neighbouring churches and the head teacher. We received encouragement from all these, though opposition from the school caretaker. We also asked for a volunteer team to shoulder the burden of organizing the new congregation. Finally we were given the go-ahead from the church annual meeting.

In September we delivered a leaflet through each door in the area, advertising the opening service. In October we set up the trestle table covered with a fine white linen cloth and decorated with a beautiful new frontal, patiently made by one of our Readers. The lectern was a music-stand, but its matching pulpit fall disguised this effectively. Before the service we gathered for prayer; and then we lit the candle and waited.

Would anyone come? To our surprise we soon had a respectably full hall, half of whom were new faces, soon to become familiar friends. Why did they come? Some were elderly people who could not walk all the way to the parish church and were so pleased that we had made the effort to come to them. Others were those who found the idea of 'church' threatening and who appreciated the informality of the school hall. Some were wanting to be involved in a new project and use their gifts. Others just came to try us out.

We began by having three teams who took it in turn to be responsible for the worship. Each was headed up by an authorized leader (clergy or Reader) and contained others who contributed their particular gifts in music, drama, praying and so on. The service was recognizably Anglican and liturgical, which is important when people move round the country so frequently. But it was also brief enough to make room for the spontaneous and the local.

The exciting thing was to see a genuine new worshipping community emerging. Adults came to faith. Others who had stopped coming to church years before restarted. I shall never forget the man who said he didn't come to church because he couldn't forgive the Japanese who had tortured his brother in the war; when he was confirmed, having found the cross after all those years, it was a real celebration. Children had an important place from week one. The worship was all-age at first, with a crèche in the corridor, so it could be noisy at times.

Of course we had problems all the way. Sunday mornings were a rush for those on duty in two places. There was no proper storage space for all the equipment. A more serious difficulty was that the school forbade access in half-terms or holidays. Hardest of all was the weight of the work, which in the early days fell on very few people. It took only a couple of families to be away for the weekend and the congregation seemed very sparse. This was depressing for those who had made the sacrifice of leaving the lively St Mary Bredin services and youth work. Some people had deliberately moved into the area and for them it was hard when things did not work as fast as they had hoped.

But there was also plenty to encourage us. It was clear from week one that it was possible to create an atmosphere of Spirit-filled worship in a school hall and there were many moving moments. The gospel is all about new beginnings, and starting a new congregation allowed us the excitement of being pioneers. The project was an excellent proving ground for those with gifts who would either find it difficult to contribute in a large congregation or would not fit in with the somewhat inflexible Anglican pattern of authorization straightaway. We had the blessing of the bishop to experiment, and experiment we did. After two years we started to see steady growth and answers to prayer. We were given proper storage space, rooms for the children, and access 52 weeks a year. After another couple of years we had to buy more chairs for the school. One of our Readers became chairman of governors and the networking of a Christian community started to become more effective. We discovered that we were part of a national phenomenon called church planting.[16]

Newcomers soon made up the gaps in the parish church, and we were forced to grow new leaders. We discovered that if you have a full church you miss out on much potential because you do not have to take risks with leadership. An unexpected bonus was the number of people coming to the evening service from both ends of the parish because they missed their friends. All this encouraged us to go ahead with our other project to build an extension to the parish church. For the second time in ten years we were uncomfortably full and began to pray about a fourth morning service.

There were, however, longer-term problems. Colleagues experienced in church planting suggested that to succeed the project needed a properly designated leader. The curates who came every four years were each highly gifted, but they came to be trained and, particularly in their first year, it was not appropriate for them to assume leadership of a congregation. The project had anyway been designed to be led mainly by a lay team. We spent much time trying unsuccessfully to clarify the relationship between assistant clergy and lay leadership. Although there was much hard work, significantly the prayer life of the congregation never took off in the way that we hoped.

I was confident that with patience we would be able to see these problems through as we had the initial ones, but then suddenly I was asked to leave the parish. The difficulties of a year-long interregnum plus some painful personality clashes brought the problems to the surface and the PCC decided to end the project and bring as many people as possible back to the mother church, overfull though it was.

Was it all a waste of energy? No. We were clearly led by God into the project, and he will lead the parish into fresh ways of being church appropriate to the next millennium. More people came back to the parish church than had left 11 years before. In business we are used to organizations regrouping, tearing down and rebuilding frequently. The early Church was much more flexible than we are. So is the Church in much of the rest of the world. Pioneering a new congregation was a great privilege. We saw the development of many ministries and leaders and the training of many disciples. There was wonderful love and mutual support in time of illness and personal tragedy. I was made to face some of my own failures in leadership. Above all it showed us that there are all sorts of people who want to worship – people we were unaware of. The division between 'unchurched' and 'dechurched' in urban areas is less sharp in practice than the theory might lead us to believe.

In all this the calling of the church leaders is to teach a vision of the Church as part of God's purpose. 'See to it (*episkopeo*) that no one fail to obtain the grace of God', says the writer to the Hebrews.[17] To see the local church as part of the catholic (world-wide), and apostolic (missionary) Church is *episkope*; that is, seeing over the heads of the immediate problems and sensing what the Church is being called to become. This is to be liberated from a burden of guilt that makes doing evangelism like dieting after Christmas, and turns it into the joyful bearing witness to what Christ is doing in our lives.

The task of the leadership team is not to make evangelism a separate function but to have an evangelistic edge to everything the local church does. The question to keep asking is, 'Is our church good news to our community and the networks we serve? Does it embody the good news of Jesus Christ it proclaims?' As St Paul remarked long ago, there is no law against a community that is seeking to be transformed in love and joy and peace.[18] In the end evangelism is about the presence of Christ at work in us. He will not leave us as we are or where we are, and his Spirit will encourage us to go where there is need and where his love is not known.

8
Managing People

STYLES OF MANAGEMENT

Hornblower walked along to his cabin; the moving cogs in the complex machine that was a ship always needed lubrication, and it was a captain's duty to see that it was provided.

C. S. Forester[1]

One of my training vicars had been an officer in the Royal Navy, and after difficult church meetings he used to mutter to himself that he wished that his obstreperous church council members were on his quarterdeck; then they would jump to it!

The armed forces and many commercial organizations have pyramidal hierarchies, which are designed to respond quickly to crises. If enemy tanks crowd over the horizon it is no good calling a committee meeting; the command must be given and obeyed without question. Of course the command will not always be right, but at least a decision is taken and put into action. In a local church, however, the troops are volunteers and serve in their spare time. When they invest time and energy without pay over the years there is also a large emotional stake. If their work has been going badly and family life is a disappointment then it is all the more important to them that the church committee goes well. Woe betide the new vicar who tries to change things faster than they can cope with!

I have known several able and confident executives who have decided in midlife to give the church the benefit of their experience and have been ordained in the mistaken belief that running a local church will be easy after the demands of a large commercial organization. Unfortunately when everyone is a volunteer and all are equal it is a different game altogether. The cogs still have to be oiled, but they also have to be consulted; otherwise they take themselves off pretty smartly, or set solid.

Collaborative ministry and democracy are time-consuming. All those caught up in synodical systems ask themselves frequently if it is a sensible use of time to take so many gifted people away from their lives to debate small points of liturgy and canon law to a standstill. Sometimes Christians from Free Church and Anglican streams look enviously at the new community churches where the 'apostles' are reputed to control everything, or towards the Roman Church where the church council is only advisory and the priest still keeps most of the power. A friend asked a Catholic priest to introduce him to the parish council; the priest replied, 'You're looking at him!' The justification for this approach is the inter- pretation of Ephesians 4.16 that says that the 'ligaments' in the body are the clergy.[2] This is the right passage of Scripture but an improbable interpretation:

But speaking [or, better, 'doing' or 'living'] the truth in love, we must grow up in every way into him who is the head, into Christ, from whom the whole body, joined and knitted together by every ligament with which it is equipped, as each part is working properly, promotes the body's growth in building itself up in love. (NRSV)

To make the clergy the joints *tout court* (whether of the Catholic sacramental sort or the Protestant teaching sort) is to reduce the calling of the people of God so severely as to undermine the rest of the New Testament. Christ called all his disciples to follow him and become part of the new family of God. There is no artificial split between the managers and the managed, any more than between the teachers and the taught or the leaders and the led in the body of Christ. Because the Christian Church is a human as well as a divine institution, there is much to learn from the management structures of the armed forces, colleges, hospitals and commercial companies. But these need evaluating by Christian standards and using lightly rather than uncritically. We can only teach when we are ourselves teachable, lead when we know what it is to follow, manage when we are under authority, in a body that is building itself up in love.

MAKING LEADERS THROUGH
ADULT LEARNING

A particular challenge in churches is how to release gifts of lay leadership in a way that other church members will accept. Why is it in church life that there is such a fine line between good, clear leading and manipulating or bullying?

In my forties Jane persuaded me to take up skiing. My first skiing holiday had the merit of being so terrifying that it completely drove all the problems of the parish out of my mind! But, reflecting on the experience afterwards, it also raised questions about how adults learn and lead. On the ski slopes we were divided into groups led by young ski instructors, who demonstrated how to do various manoeuvres and then ordered us over dauntingly steep slopes to try them for ourselves. We fell over repeatedly. They told us that a ski champion is only someone who never tires of falling over, but it was bruising. However, after a few days we fell over less frequently and began to find the slopes exhilarating. We started to master some of the manoeuvres and even learned in a rudimentary way to stop.

My questions were: How did those young instructors enable us to do all that, when in church if leaders try to persuade us to do anything out of the ordinary we rebel? Why do people find being shouted at by a ski instructor while wobbling embarrassingly in front of a group of their peers helpful, when the same kind of approach in a church meeting would be perceived as bullying? Are there things that church leaders can learn from ski instructors?

This last question is easier to answer than the others. A good ski instructor has to have infinite patience and has to break the manoeuvres down into separate steps. It would be easy for her to say to me, 'You look terrible. If you carry on like that you will never learn!' But she never does; she says, 'Well done, Jonathan; you're doing A right, and B is coming on well. Next time I want you to firm up B, and will you also have a go at C.' The instruction stretches you, does not compromise on the reality of the steepness of the slope, but breaks the learning down into sufficiently small steps so that you can see yourself improving. So I learn because the lesson is in achievable steps, because there is constant, warm but objective encouragement and criticism, and because I feel safe in a hazardous place. Adults learn readily in churches too where they are stretched by definite but achievable learning projects, where there is constant encouragement and where disciples feel safe to take risks.

Other reasons why I learn are more difficult to transfer directly to the church. I am such a beginner and the instructors are so far ahead that I have to watch the instructor demonstrate how it is done; I learn through clear modelling. These things are more complicated in churches, where we are interested not just in techniques but in character. An instructor at a local church may be a brilliant preacher but have a sharp temper, may be full of the Spirit but (like the Corinthians) immature. Our chief instructor is of course Jesus Christ and it is to him that we have to turn for the clear modelling.

On our first skiing trip we had instruction in the mornings and free skiing in the afternoons when we beginners went off together and practised what we had learned in the morning. Although none of us was much good we had different levels of confidence. One person was afraid to go on a T-bar lift alone; another wanted to go down a particular slope but could not cope with part of it. In each case we found we could manage the difficulty if someone with more confidence accompanied us. He or she would say, 'I can't instruct you, but I can accompany you and help you.' For many aspects of Christian leadership that is a more appropriate model than the ski instructor. In a balanced life the Christian will move in and out of leading and being led, accompanying and being accompanied. When Jesus and Paul trained their disciples they adapted the common discipling methods of the rabbis of their time. Today churches have a responsibility to provide a variety of frameworks for Christian adult learning appropriate to our time.

A CHURCH STRATEGY AND VISION

During our various building projects it was noticeable how people pulled together, how they took pride in achieving things, how they put themselves out for the common good. When we were not building it was more difficult. The problem about much church life is that we are dealing with the invisible and the ineffable. You cannot quantify growth in holiness at the annual general meeting. That is of course as it should be, and to reduce a church to a local business with a business plan would be to empty it of its purpose.[3] Nevertheless a church is not only part of God's eternal mission; it is also a corporate body with the usual characteristics and needs of an organization. One set of needs is to have clear intermediate and achievable goals, which can be owned by members and which can provide the context for particular ministries. I cannot ask someone to take over the chair of the mission action group, for instance, without providing a brief that starts with the church policy on mission.

Where does a church strategy come from? It is a complex and exciting process. In the Old Testament God reveals his will to his prophets, giving them his word, and telling them to confront his people with his demands. One of the ways in which strategy still starts is through the prophetic preaching of God's word. In the historical books we see God leading his people, stretching their faith through the toughening up process of their experiences of bondage, exile and deliverance. Today, too, strategy emerges as a result of a congregation being stretched through various faith exercises; through the sickness and death of key members, through miracles and answers to prayer. In the New Testament, Jesus battles with Satan in the wilderness over the difference between a superficial strategy of signs-and-wonders and a tougher one that follows the way of the cross; we see him spending nights in prayer over significant choices such as the calling of the twelve. Still today a church will be faced with competing visions, some of them seductive; and Christian goal-setting without awareness of the battle in the heavenlies is cutting corners. Is it coincidental that the churches that seem to take big risks and achieve great things are the churches that organize nights of prayer and days of fasting? In the New Testament we can see both Jesus and Paul laying down plans for mission, for covering the ground, for training and sending out disciples, for follow-up and reflection on mission work. It is an interesting exercise to study the interruptions that met Jesus on the way to Jerusalem and how he dealt with them;

patiently allowing people's pain and suffering to delay him, and yet not permitting other people's agendas to deflect him from God's call. There are both flexibility and ruthlessness in the Lord's strategy.

In the Acts and Epistles there is a constant tension between human planning, the cussedness of people and events, and the intervention of the Spirit in prophecy, dreams and healings. Acts 16 is a fascinating cameo of how carefully thought-out strategies are cast aside and a far greater enterprise (the first step in the evangelization of Europe) undertaken at the prompting of the Spirit. In Acts 13 the congregational leaders fast and wait upon God for the fitting of people and tasks together. Still today a strategy without the right people in the right posts is useless, but strategies pour out once the right people are in place.

In our parish we have a church vision document, which came out of much prayer and discussion with church leaders and the church council. It is printed on the inside cover of the church telephone book so that everyone has a copy for reference, and it is given to all taking on a new ministry. Then we have various applications of the vision for particular areas of work: for the youth work, for example, or the choir and band. Neither the church vision nor the various policy documents are permanent; rather they are snapshots of a church that is moving on. Every couple of years or so we discover that some part is out of date and needs to be modified.

It is against the background of a church struggling to grow and change in obedience to the Spirit that other more concrete goals are determined and decisions made; all the fascinating details of church life from installing new gas heaters in the church hall to holding a holiday club for children. One of the great advantages of having in place a vision and strategy that are inspiring and demanding is that other decisions can be put into perspective and the whole decision-making process can be cooler and calmer. We have all had the experience of tiny decisions assuming huge importance in church councils and committees. When a church is excited about moving forward, even quite major decisions can safely be put into the hands of officers and working parties, and church councils can debate and pray about matters of principle and longer-term policy rather than spending interminable meetings on whether or not to move the bookstall.

MANAGING RELATIONSHIPS

The most precious resource that the Church has, after the presence of God himself and his word, is surely people. And yet churches are not conspicuously successful in treasuring and employing that resource. At any gathering of lay Christians if you ask about lay ministry you hear sad stories about clergy stifling lay initiative. Many of the accounts do not stand up to closer examination but, after taking all the mitigating factors into account, there is still a residue of complaint that suggests that we are failing to spot leadership and ministry potential, and failing to support and train. Clergy do not have much power to make things happen, but we have large powers of veto – negative power that can blight lives and hold back the growth of the church.

No minister begins by wanting his parish or diocese to serve him or her. We all start by longing to serve the people in our care. But, partly because of the weakness in our own lives, and partly because of the structures and burden of office, we find ourselves under pressure, then failing to listen or pick up the signs, and finally harming those in our charge. It may well be that the failure of our churches to evangelize the nation has as much to do with our treatment of one another within the Church as a failure of mission strategy or lack of prayer. To put it more bluntly, the nation might sit up and take notice of a church that was more successful in using the gifts of its members.

Managing people is simply a way of loving them. When my parish priest spends a morning writing letters, that is bureaucracy; when he writes *me* a letter, that is pastoral care. Jesus organized the five thousand into groups to feed them. In the same way, pastoral care depends on proper organization. A parish that is not well managed is uncared for. Of course the values of a large commercial organization may be quite different from those of the kingdom of God; the goals will almost certainly be. But without proper managing we cannot properly love people. Unless 'each part is working properly' bodily growth does not happen.

ALLOWING OTHER LEADERS TO FLOURISH

The experienced pastor quickly recognizes that offers of help can sometimes lead to big trouble. A new arrival in church expresses an interest in helping with something that really wants doing: running the bookstall, or teaching the class of 11-year-olds. For a few months the new person is obliging in every respect, turns up to tasks and meetings that almost no one else comes to and takes on the proposed area of ministry with vision and zeal. Within 12 months, however, a terrible alteration takes place. The now not-so-new arrival is no longer so co-operative; on the contrary you are expected to fit the church programme round the area of ministry that has become a separate fiefdom. And short of a terrible row, which bruises everyone and half-destroys the bookstall or the class of 11-year-olds, it is difficult to reclaim things for the church.

This is such a well-known phenomenon among clergy that it deserves close attention. To start with it sets up a vicious cycle. Pastors once bitten become twice shy and start turning away offers of help from competent and enthusiastic Christians. This is a wonderful device of the Devil to stop what the church needs more than most things, which is an explosion of lay leadership. The result is that potential lay ministers find the priest or pastor difficult to help and he soon gets a partly deserved reputation for being a one-man-band who wants to hang on to all ministry, with the result that growth stops and competent people leave. Soon the church levels down to the size that the minister can cope with.

C. T. Studd is a good example of how badly we can go wrong in this area, of how a brilliant leader can do untold damage if he is not corrected. In the 1880s Charles Studd was known as the most eligible bachelor in England, heir to a fortune and the nation's captain of cricket. He gave it all up to be a missionary in China. He did outstanding work and captured the imagination of all who supported overseas mission, but he was extremely difficult to work with because he would in practice be under no one. The directors of the China Inland Mission complained that he would not take advice and Hudson Taylor himself wrote of him, 'He is too independent.'[4] In his fifties he took a trip up the Nile and decided to evangelize the unreached tribes of Africa. The Church Missionary

Society showed him round South Sudan but he decided he could not work with Anglicans. So he joined the Africa Inland Mission instead. But, three weeks after signing this mission's constitution, he asked that it be changed so that he could have complete independence in appointing his own people and handling his own finances. When the AIM decided against changing its constitution at the behest of its newest recruit he resigned immediately.[5] Studd did not want to be managed. On the other hand when Studd was in command he had to be obeyed.[6] The tragedy about him was that in theory he knew and taught that Christians should be submissive to those in authority; but in practice marched to a different tune. 'Speaking the truth in love' has to include the kind of toughness that allows local leadership proper room for manoeuvre but is not afraid to set boundaries, to confront wrong and to nip trouble in the bud so that others may flourish.

The key to all this is that every Christian leader is called to be good at leading, collaborating, consulting and being led. All of us are naturally better at one or the other of these, but we are called to practise all and to grow and develop our skills in all. Jesus commended the Roman centurion because he demonstrated that he was under authority, and Jesus himself modelled what it meant to obey when it was painful. Many Christians, including many Christian leaders, model the kind of anarchy that obeys only when it sees fit.

MANAGING TIME AND SELF

There is something about the unstructured nature of parochial ministry that encourages us clergy to become obsessive and then to overwork. It is deeply ironic that we who ostensibly live from proclaiming God's grace and strength within us, fall into working as if it all depended upon us, with the result that our behaviour undermines our gospel.

The full-time employee of a local church starts with a blank diary and a series of questions about his or her role. Very often curates, youth workers, administrators and pastoral assistants feel guilty about the empty afternoons and wonder how to fill them.

Sometimes they take on new projects with enthusiasm and energy to justify their employment. After a few months the opposite problem starts to overwhelm; after a year exhaustion sets in and either there has to be a fresh appraisal or a life of chaos and bad habits is embarked upon. I once worked for a vicar who dictated his letters for his children to his secretary – and she put in the bits he had forgotten. I have known many ministers and clergy at all levels who have moved from engagement to engagement, saying a few words here and there without proper preparation and hoping that no one will notice (they will) and exasperating their lay colleagues. At worst they become preoccupied with their own role, fail to listen or see what is happening around them and start simply reacting to circumstances.

An oft-repeated management parable has a woman walking into a forest and spotting a man exhausting himself by attempting to cut down trees with a blunt saw. 'Why don't you sharpen the saw?' she asks naively. 'Because I haven't got time,' answers the man.

Often I have worked myself into the situation where I have known myself to be overloaded and where there is no easy escape. The sermons have to be prepared, the dying have to be visited, the problem in the choir cannot be put off, the scouts are demanding a meeting, and even the diocesan forms cannot be left for another week. At such times helpful hints from time-management experts are simply infuriating or discouraging. Under those circumstances I have known some heart-searching because my wife and family have suffered, and I have had to work through my timetable again from scratch, admitting that extra responsibilities have been taken on for the wrong reasons and have unbalanced the programme, and that rigorous pruning is necessary. But how? On more than one occasion Psalm 8 has come like a word from heaven, encouraging me to take control of my life again and not to give in:

> When I look at your heavens, the work of your fingers,
> the moon and the stars that you have established;
> what are human beings that you are mindful of them,
> mortals that you care for them?
> Yet you have made them a little lower than God,

and crowned them with glory and honour.
You have given them dominion over the works of your hands;
you have put all things under their feet.

(Psalm 8.3–6, NRSV)

If God has given us dominion, this must include control over my timetable: I must be able to have a timetable that honours him and gives due place to my family and friends, a schedule that acknowledges my position as a child of God in relationship with others, and does not reduce me to a cog in an ecclesiastical machine.

MANAGING MEETINGS

Meetings are marvellous opportunities for that coming together of minds and hearts which enables all sorts of things to be achieved. But meetings are normally wasted opportunities. There are five common problems with committee meetings and, if several of these are present at once, the meeting will soon run itself into the sand.

1 *Lack of clear purpose*. Many committees were set up for some purpose which is no longer clear.
2 *Too many members*. No one ever complains that committees are too small. But frequently a committee is too large for it to work effectively.
3 *Lack of preparation*. I have sat year after year on committees where the chairman has rushed into the room and said (in words or by body language), 'Which meeting are we in today?' while the members quietly fume.
4 *Overloaded agenda*. Committees often get lost in detail, so meetings go on for longer than the subject-matter warrants.
5 *Difficult people*. We all have off days, but sometimes church committees seem to have off people. This may be because things are wrong elsewhere in their lives and they are transferring that frustration.

Where these problems are tackled then the Ephesians vision becomes more of a reality.

I A CLEAR PURPOSE

Meetings have purposes and aims at many different levels. First, a committee will have a general aim or vision. For instance, the purpose of a parochial church council (PCC) is 'to co-operate with the incumbent in the whole mission of the church, pastoral and evangelistic'.[7] As members change after the annual meeting it is important for a fresh statement of the purpose and nature of a PCC to be given by the chairman, and from time to time during the year the meeting will need a gentle reminder of the general aim. Second, each separate meeting will also have its aims. If there is no real purpose to a particular meeting, then cancel it. Everyone will be able to use the time more profitably. Third, a meeting is a meeting with people; some thought needs to be given to the growing relationships and balance of people, those chosen for their expertise and those for their general wisdom or weight in the community. Fourth, a Christian meeting should be planned as a meeting with God as well as with one another. It is true that a PCC which regularly begins with a Communion service or a long peroration will make the members think that the vicar is trying to soften them up. (Sometimes he is.) But committee meetings that include worship and prayer will focus people's minds on purposes beyond the parochial; business meetings can be inspiring and uplifting, as people come to decisions and achieve things beyond what they thought themselves capable. An 'away day' to discuss the performance of the committee and its success and failure in reaching its aims is useful, particularly if a consultant can be brought in to help.

2 SIZE

Different kinds of meeting need to be of different sizes. Sub-committees and task forces of three to four members work well at creative tasks. Five to ten can do some creative work or carry a task forward. With 15 and above a different dynamic starts to operate, where discussion has to be more carefully controlled by the chair; and meetings of over 30 members will have factions and depend on able speakers and powerful personalities. In some small churches the PCC or equivalent is in effect the meeting of all the active worshipping members (and often some inactive ones as well!); it is thus the main meeting for fellowship as well as for business. But if the church grows it will be important to separate the two functions. Charles Handy makes the helpful point that committees are different from teams. Teams, he maintains, are groups of people who are there with a shared and common purpose, but committees are representative and hold the accountability of an organization.[8]

3 PREPARATION

The chairman and secretary (or for larger organizations the standing committee or agenda sub-committee) will want to spend some time in preparing the agenda. When I first started going to PCCs the main agenda usually looked like this.

Vicar's Reflections
Secretary
Wardens' Report
Treasurer's Report
Report on the Fabric
Deanery Synod
Any Other Business

It made the agenda look short, and it saved paper, but no one could do any preparation. It assumed a passive membership (though old hands know that behind AOB lurks many a possibility for alarm and despondency at 9.59 p.m.). Who knows if the 'Fabric Report' means that a light bulb has blown or the church tower is falling down; if we are merely to be informed that the gate has been repainted or if we are going to be asked to hire a new gardener? What are the main decisions to be made at the meeting? Are there items that I need to prepare or to ask people about?

As much as possible decisions should be prepared for in the agenda. So a notice of meeting will look more like this:

Meeting on Thursday 6 November from 7.30 to 9.30 p.m.

1 Opening Worship
2 Apologies, Minutes, Matters arising

3 Personnel

Jill Ash is being proposed for the new Diocesan Ministry Training Course and will ask the PCC to support her application.

4 Outreach

Discussion item. Jesse will report on the parish visiting and float a scheme for street wardens to be shared with the Council of Churches.

5 Secretary

The Baptist church has invited us to join them on Maundy Thursday evening for a Passover Meal (see enclosed proposal). Do we accept?

6 Time of Prayer

7 Treasurer's Report

First quarter figures (enclosed), plus a proposal to buy a scanner for the church office.

8 Report on the Fabric

The Fabric Committee will report that everything major on the quinquennial inspection has now been undertaken and will suggest that the PCC delegates to them the arrangements for the Rural Dean's inspection.

In this way people know what is to be decided and will come prepared. Different people will speak to each item. Even with well-signalled advance notice it is usually inadvisable to ask a meeting to decide anything major in one go. I have often regretted making this mistake myself and seen others do it too. Major decisions need at least two bites at the cherry.

4 THE BALANCE OF THE AGENDA

Another important matter to consider is the balance of the meeting. It is better to have one good discussion and make one or two important decisions than to have a series of hurried items. Over the course of a year it is wise to include matters that inform, inspire and encourage alongside the business items. But the people have come to decide, not just to be talked at, or to have discussions that never lead to decision. It is the task of the chairman and secretary to time the meeting. I have often sat in meetings where the first three-quarters of the allotted time have been spent on some obscure legal point that expanded uncontrollably, and the item on evangelism or the new youth structure has had to be dealt with at the end or put off for another time.

5 A THEOLOGY OF FLOURISHING

It was said of Kevin Keegan, when manager of Newcastle United, that 'Those coming under his influence have given the impression of men liberated, relieved of pressure, able to enjoy work. "We never dwell on what they're not good at. Maybe that's the secret."'[9] Church meetings can be great opportunities of enabling people to grow into new roles. Where there is a theology of flourishing, people can be stretched and achieve things beyond what they thought was their capacity. Where there is defensiveness and competitiveness the opposite obtains.

Nelson Mandela writes in his autobiography of how he learned about leadership from the way in which decisions were made in the African villages of his childhood. A minority was not to be crushed by a majority. Meetings would continue until a consensus was reached. The skill of the leader was, while putting up with sometimes fierce criticism without defending himself, to encourage others to speak, and then to sum up wisely what had been said and to form some kind of consensus.[10]

MANAGING DIFFICULTIES

Like every human community a church will have an atmosphere, an ethos, which is more than the sum of its parts. It will be partly a result of its history, largely a result of the prayers of previous generations, sometimes affected by factors that defy our analysis. We clergy are frequently baffled by the way that people behave; but we, of all people, should not be surprised if spiritual forces are at work.

One of the more obvious causes of spiritual disturbance in a church is a leader who has let the church down morally. A treasurer who has purloined the funds, an organist who has interfered with choristers, a vicar who has had an affair with a member of the congregation can have a deleterious effect for years after the event. That would perhaps be clear if the failure were widely known. What is sometimes mysterious is that when hardly any one knows of the fault or crime this effect still lingers and can cloud the atmosphere of the church for a decade. It is not always easy to know how to deal with such a problem. A new vicar who unearths the fact that the treasurer before last had misappropriated some funds has a puzzle on his hands. The treasurer is long gone, the wardens dealt with it as best they could – the last thing we want to do is to give it publicity. And yet, every time the new vicar preaches about stewardship and tithing a gloom seems to settle over the congregation; although they do not know what happened, it seems as if on an unconscious level they are replying to the preacher, 'We cannot trust this church with our money, so we are not going to give.'

Over the years I have noticed that the tendency among the clergy is to hope that a new start will do the trick and to trust that the effect of the sin of the previous generation will fade with time. Perhaps sometimes it does, but in several neighbouring churches I have observed that often it does not and more direct action is needed. First, it is important to pray for guidance with one or two trusted church officials and to listen carefully to any prophetic insight or revelation that might be given. Second, it is good to remember that Christians are called to 'walk in the light' as much as possible, and it is Satan who tries to keep us from dealing openly and honestly with one another. I remember a case where a woman confessed a misdemeanour but insisted that nothing was done about it because she did not want her husband to know. This tied the hands of the church leader – unnecessarily, as it later turned out, because the husband had known all along anyway. As so often the real problem was not the obvious sin but the web of deception involved. Third and most important, the Lord himself teaches us to go directly to the person who has sinned and talk about it face to face. Matthew 18 is all about community discipline, and the principle of going to see the person who has wronged the community face to face is usually the right thing to do. At the very least it gives the other person a chance to defend him- or herself against what may be unfounded gossip. Fourth, not all problems have to be dealt with at once. It is good to have wise senior colleagues with whom one can discuss things in a measured way so that Satan cannot manoeuvre us too quickly on to ground of his choosing.[11]

Different management styles are appropriate to different sizes and types of church. There is no necessary conflict between the 'spiritual' and the 'managerial'. Being part of a community where pastoral care is properly organized, where people's time is not wasted, where redemption and reconciliation are practised and where wounds are being healed is to know what human beings were created for. Problems arise because the aspirations are usually higher in a church than in a commercial enterprise, but humans are still prone to jealousy, insecurity and competitiveness. But if management is seen as a way of loving people more effectively, if encouragement is management's chief tool and if a common vision has been reached, people will gladly follow and join in the adventure of learning together how to grow up to the measure of the full stature of Christ.

9
Raising Money – Finance and Buildings

FUND-RAISING

Outside the church was an appeal board with a painted ther-
mometer. Each month the red stripe went up a little further
towards the goal of £20,000. It seemed an immense amount of
money at the time and it was exciting to see the red stripe moving
upwards, but as I passed this church regularly I couldn't help
worrying. The other notice-board welcomed newcomers and
invited them to come and worship, but was quite dwarfed by the
appeal board. 'If God is so mighty,' I reasoned as a teenager, 'then
why does he let the roof of his local church fall down to the extent
that an appeal has to be made to the general public?' Does his
church need to be propped up by the unbelieving (or at least
non-churchgoing) populace?

Since then I have learned that the question is more complex
and that there are legitimate reasons for appealing for money from
the non-churchgoing inhabitants. For instance, a medieval village
church, it can be argued, belongs to the whole village. It con-
tributes immeasurably to the skyline and to the village green, it is
used for village functions and for rites of passage; in short it is
generally understood that the village as well as the worshippers
should contribute to its upkeep. If the church has architectural
merit, repair costs will be huge but money can also be obtained
from the Department of the Environment or English Heritage.

But even here the worshippers will want to exercise caution. If
the village pays for the church it will rightly want a say in its
decoration and especially in any changes made. The village, or
powerful voices within it, may not see it at all as a building that has
changed over the centuries, adapted to the current needs of the

people of God.[1] On the contrary the line from the hymn, 'but nothing changes here', may well be their rallying cry, and even the very reason why they moved into the village. For many occasional churchgoers, the building stands for those values that should not change, in the midst of a world which is full of change for its own sake. Colleagues who have accepted money from preservation charities have found out that it can mean signing away for ever the possibility of making changes to the building without their approval.

The urban or suburban church, unless it is a town-centre building of unusual merit, will be largely ignored by or unknown to the non-churchgoing population. Here it is not only ineffective to appeal for money from them but also dangerous. It will plant in their minds the idea that the church is only after their money; whereas they 'know' that the Church Commissioners have millions to spare, and the Vatican is full of gold. It will prejudice them against any other kind of outreach that the local church decides upon.

FÊTE WORSE THAN DEATH?

Another part of local church life is sales of work, fêtes, bazaars and auctions. In theory these are fun, bring people together, use talents for knitting and making jam that would otherwise have no outlet, and raise sums of money for good causes. Certainly I have been to events – and even helped organize them – that have lived up to these ideals. But there is another side which is less good.

First of all, a fête can give to the organizers and purchasers the idea that they have done their duty as far as Christian giving is concerned, and can even have the overall effect of reducing the income of the church in a community.

Second, all fund-raising efforts are hard work and take time. The church council needs to think through the strategy of how much time and energy people have to spare and whether it is most effective to use it in this way. My own experience is that it is not. I visited a church recently where, in order to maintain the beautiful building, there was a weekly sale of work and coffee morning. I could not think it was a coincidence that the vicar was recovering from a heart attack and his wife (who catered for the event each week) at her wits' end. It was incidentally a fairly prosperous community, but its heart had not been touched by the church. I have been to other churches where the congregation was harangued in the notices for not turning up in sufficient numbers to support the fête. Fund-raising is a great way to turn the joy of Christian receiving and giving into an endless round of guilt.

Third, the annual sale of work can become at best a tired and outmoded tradition that needs killing off, and at worst a power base for a group of people who have found a way of sidestepping the gospel. 'Vicar, Mr Jones has put his second-hand bookstall right by the door. You must know that for the last 20 years I have had my raffle for the League of Pity there' is the all-too-common remark that faces the new minister on his first visit to the sale and makes him think longingly of working down a salt-mine in Siberia.

Fourth, church sales and fund-raising can be a seat of self-delusion. There was a woman who used to buy ballpoint pens for 12p and sell them 'cheap' at the church fête for 10p, and no amount of explanation could convince her that she would have done better to put the original purchase money quietly into the collection.

It is not surprising that Jesus spoke of Mammon not in a neutral way but as a power that can invade human hearts and entrap. It is obvious that our culture has been ensnared. What will the future think of a generation that put its very best artistic talent into creating publicity for selling rival brands of dog food or lavatory paper on TV? It is a tragedy if the Church also becomes confused. In some places fund-raising has become like couch grass in a garden, stifling the good growth of the gospel in the church's life. In other places the good has become the enemy of the best and people are simply too tired by supporting the good works to see that the Church of Christ has a better approach to offer. So how do we raise funds for the local church and for all the charitable and missionary projects that call upon us? The answer is simple and it works!

PRINCIPLES OF GIVING

Church people often complain about the expense of keeping a church going; especially if things are organized centrally as they are in the Anglican Church where everyone pays a 'quota' to the diocese, which is then shared out to the parishes as clergy stipends. Every year parish treasurers and clergy meet the diocesan officials and complain that there is no more money in the parish and it is quite impossible to raise the quota. Then somehow or other we do raise it, just, and the whole process starts over again.

What cured me of that once and for all was the experience of attending the annual general meeting of a working men's club. The electoral roll of the parish church was the same size as the membership of the working men's club. The parish population was very mixed, but those who came to church and contributed to the giving scheme were decidedly more middle-class than the club members. I was interested to note that the income of the working men's club was almost exactly the same as that of the parish church. *We* preached annually on the need for sacrificial giving in the church in order to pay the quota. *They* raised all their money on two fruit machines and the profits from the bar. Suddenly the penny dropped. *We* went through a great performance each year, claiming that we were responding to God with sacrifice in our worship. *They* raised the same amount, out of a fraction of their leisure spending, without any exhortations and certainly without any sense of it being given away. I could only conclude that the protestations of poverty from the churches were partly self-delusion.

Like many parishes we have a finance team who support the treasurer against an increasingly complex fiscal background. They help to organize a Commitment Sunday each autumn. Three weeks in advance, they ask the preaching team to preach on the Christian principles of giving and suitable Old and New Testament readings are chosen. This is the only occasion during the year when an appeal for money is made from the pulpit, and even here the primary emphasis is on the good news of a generous God. Leaflets explaining the church budget for the following year and various possibilities of giving are distributed, and a member of the finance team is available after each of the services to explain to individuals how the tax system works. We discover through this that many do not understand the practicalities and would like to give but are scared of what would happen if their financial situation should change. The team explain our arrangements for releasing anyone from a promise should redundancy or some other disaster strike. Everyone is asked to pray about his or her giving for the following year and to return a pledge on Commitment Sunday, offering it as part of the worship. From time to time we have half-nights of prayer when there are special financial needs to be met but, apart from these and the explanation of the accounts at the annual general meeting, finance is able to stay in the background.

Because of this we have not had to have a series of fund-raising events for the church, but have been able to support uniformed organizations and other good causes locally in their efforts. For instance, a group of church members runs a stall in aid of the local county primary school at the school fair. We have a family who organize an annual sale to raise money for a specific charity; it is held in the church hall and many church members support it, and it is a great success, but it is a private initiative rather than a church one. In one church I worked in there was a fine missionary sale once a year at which gardeners exchanged plants, people made and sold things, there were games and other amusements for the children. But it was clearly understood first that this was the only such event in the church calendar, and second that all money was to be spent away from the local church on charities and missions. In this way it did not get tangled up in people's minds with tithing.

I recently visited two neighbouring parishes which, coincidentally, were raising money during the same weekend. The first was holding its traditional autumn fayre. The church hall had a musty smell and the bric-a-brac and home-knitted goods were of low quality for a prosperous area. Weeks of work produced less than £1,000 profit. Their neighbours held a gift day for church members. It was a much poorer area but 25 people had pledged £35,000.

SPECIAL PROJECTS

THE REBUILDING OF ST GEORGE'S

Often a special project can teach a congregation the gospel principles about God's provision in a most striking way. We have all heard of people praying for money and the anonymous cheque for just the right amount dropping through the door; but when it happens to you and publicly in a church family, the miracles are much more exciting.

By 1980, two years after we moved to St George's, Folkestone, the church was full to overflowing. It was an area of new mixed housing, rented and privately owned. Our predecessors were gifted and faithful parish priests and we had the privilege of reaping where they and others had sown. A recently retired Church Army sister, Helen Foster, gave the benefit of a lifetime's service as an evangelist and trainer to the church.

My incumbent, Simon Crawley, Vicar of the parish church of Holy Trinity, Folkestone, had made the strategic decision that this was the moment to free his next curate from many of his duties at the parish church and concentrate his energies at the daughter church. He was also the kind of man who delighted in building up and encouraging others, even at his own expense. Instead of looking over his shoulder to the younger families of St George's and expecting them to come and show loyalty to the parish church, Simon encouraged St George's to grow, to the extent of directing some more people to us if he thought they would appreciate our less formal services. I have never forgotten how selflessly he lived out the John the Baptist principle.

One of the questions on my heart for some years had been, 'Does the gospel actually work in middle England?' I had seen that in university towns with gifted leaders spectacular church growth was possible. But would the gospel have any effect in a settled community, a local church with ordinary leadership? God gave us an answer in Folkestone that we could not mistake.

The community used and was familiar with the dual-purpose building during the week for play school, youth clubs and organizations for young and old – most of them quietly and effectively staffed by church members. It was not too strange for the people to come back to the same building on a Sunday. We changed what had been essentially a Children's Service into a simple adult service with Sunday school, we started a 'Christian Night School' mid-week like the evening classes at the local adult education centre; and soon we saw exciting growth to the extent that it seemed like the parable of the sower come to Folkestone. Something would have to be done about our building.

Not everything was easy of course. Although we had certainly not caused the growth – it just seemed to happen – we had to cope with it; God gave us wonderful colleagues but the press of new people upon us left us frequently exhausted. That masked the fact that I was inexperienced and had a great deal of learning about God and people to do, something that Simon Crawley hinted at from time to time but was far too gracious to confront me with.

There were also external difficulties that spoke of the general loss of nerve in the church at that time. St George's was on a good corner plot in a part of Folkestone that had grown up between the wars. A large parcel of land had been given for a church and hall; in 1938 the hall was built, but the war came and the projected church building was never added. When we arrived it was still a 1930s hall, seating a squashed 150, with a stage and beyond that a tiny, damp sanctuary. As we walked through the main doors we smelt the disinfectant from the lavatories as we passed – hardly a welcoming sign in the late 1970s.

In the early 1960s the covenanted land had been released and a row of maisonettes had been constructed on them. Then, worst of all: a new parsonage house had been built in the middle of the plot originally planned for the church. The result was that the generous provision made in the 1930s for a growing part of town had been whittled away so that little further growth on the church site was possible. It seemed a symbol of the general 1970s loss of nerve in the Church of England. There was growth, but no one saw it or believed it. I approached diocesan officials for advice and realized that if I had gone to ask about closing St George's there would have been a ready-made procedure; but no seemed to know what to do with a daughter church that was outgrowing its premises. We were a procedural embarrassment.

And ironically enough there had been growth just after the disastrous decisions had been taken, so that during the 1970s two extensions had already been added to the building, to make room for children's groups and committee meetings. But when the rapid growth in adults came at the end of the decade, it was difficult to see what could be done next on such a crowded site. Probably a radical solution would have been best – knocking down the parsonage, and freeing up the site to build a church. But the parish would not countenance anything of the sort; after all generous gifts had only recently been given so that the parsonage house could be built. And God, too, had other plans, wanting to teach us that community growth was more important than beautiful buildings. Somehow it seemed that smoothing down the rough edges on the living stones was higher on his agenda than an aesthetically pleasing building.

As the church continued to overflow we engaged an architect who devised a plan to extend the building for a third time. It was not beautiful, it would cost the then large sum of £65,000, but it would house us all in a good, flexible, dual-purpose space. It was Paul Rampton, my immediate predecessor, who had the idea that greatly improved the plans – by turning the 'nave' round by 180° and designing a new full-width sanctuary.

The question was, where would we find the money? St George's church had a tradition that money raised by fund-raising should be given away to missions; we did not want to break that tradition. Most of the congregation had joined us only recently and were not either wealthy or accustomed to giving from their income; we ourselves were on Family Income Supplement. As we had nothing to fall back on but God and his principles of giving, we started with prayer. A series of sermons on Nehemiah and rebuilding the walls of Jerusalem seemed apposite. The example of other churches that had experienced miraculous provision in the way of giving was helpful. The District Church Council was soon united behind the project. Together we designed a leaflet that would simply ask people to give from their income, covenanted over four years if possible, saying that the project would go ahead if enough people responded.

In the end there were three stages to the appeal. The first was that the major proportion of the project sum was promised by the congregation. This enabled us to go ahead with tendering and to sign a contract. The second was that we had a few couples who had retired from north London to Folkestone. While they did not care for all the noise and informality of the family service they provided some wise leadership for the church and, when they saw that the younger families were starting to give sacrificially from their incomes for the building, they in turn produced some generous pledges. Friends had warned us that we should be prepared to double the architect's estimates of both the cost and duration of the building. The overrun was not as large as that but we suddenly had to find another £10,000 to enable the project to be completed. The vicar and wardens of Holy Trinity stepped in at that point and generously made the sum available.

So it was that the bulldozers moved in to demolish the 40-year-old lavatories at last, to knock down two complete walls, and we found ourselves living on a building site. Everyone enjoyed choosing colour schemes and furnishings. A local school with a glass studio volunteered to produce a 'loaves and fishes' theme for the new sanctuary. Certainly the multiplication of our slender resources seemed not much less miraculous than the feeding of the five thousand. My own contribution was less successful. On the morning of the grand opening I decided to re-hang the large brass cross in its new place at the head of the church. As I drilled into the new plasterwork there was a loud bang – I had hit the main cable! It was good that I was wearing rubber-soled shoes and that the electrician was on hand to repair the damage.

The rebuilding of the church had quite an impact on the local community. We discovered that a new church building can help many to see that the church is alive – and somehow new people come to faith in Christ as a result. Fifteen months after the completion of the project, when Jane and I were called away to a new parish, we were accustomed to putting out over 300 chairs on a Sunday morning.

It would be good to report that the building and the church then went on from strength to strength. Sadly that was not the case. The mortar mix in the bricks was wrong; there had been some failure of supervision, and expensive repairs were necessary. More seriously, someone in the diocese had an acquaintance who had been working in a monastery and wanted to try parish life again; it was decided that our daughter church full of families was a suitable place for him. Only a few months later it became clear to both priest and people that a mismatch had been made. Those who had given so sacrificially in money and time felt bewildered, and it took years to undo the damage. Although we were only one part of the leadership team, we felt we had let everyone down by leaving. But Holy Trinity saw something of a revival as a large group of energetic younger families moved from St George's to the parish church. The generosity that Simon had shown was repaid in God's timing.

We always give thanks for the experience of that rapid church growth, for the friendships, and for the marvellous provision of money by direct giving for the expansion of the building. Certainly God had answered my question. One of the exciting things about St George's was that no one came from outside the immediate parish or further than a few hundred yards from the church. You do not need to be a city-centre, eclectic church to see growth. The gospel is the good seed that can build Christian community in ordinary mixed parishes – anywhere. For all of us who were part of St George's, Folkestone, in those years it was a lesson we will never forget.

ST MARY BREDIN

A few years later we again found ourselves having to consider a building project. The growth at St Mary Bredin Church, Canterbury, was slower but steady, and the pressure point became the number of children attending with their parents. The church hall was overflowing. We cleared out the church basement and made it into a den for the Pathfinders (aged 10 to 13). The vicarage had the crèche in the kitchen and dining room, other groups in the sitting room, hall and study. When the Sunday school leaders asked if they could start using the bedrooms we knew that something would have to be done. We settled down to pray and to dream dreams together. An architect in the congregation drew up sketch plans for a new building alongside the church, which could house an office, lavatories, a quiet room and coffee lounge as well as space for our children's work for the foreseeable future.

We had a good working party, led by people who cheerfully gave a great deal of their time over several years. We chose a local firm of architects and explored the various permissions we would need. But the estimates were for over a quarter of a million pounds. Some in the church were excited by this; others were horrified, particularly as we were already committed to a church planting project at the far end of the parish. There were some stormy open meetings and angry letters. Surely Canterbury had enough ecclesiastical buildings!

Gradually, however, as the numbers grew, the beauty and simplicity of the sketch plans convinced all but a few of the doubters. One of the chief opponents now agreed to join the extension committee. It was time for some concerted praying and the first of a regular series of gift days. Around this time tragedy struck and first our treasurer and then our deputy treasurer died of cancer, both in their early fifties. What happened next changed everything. Both widows decided to make the money they received on the death of their husbands available to the church to help finance the project. We bought a small house near the church for a few years as an investment while we saved up for the extension and put a pastoral assistant and the youth work in it. Looking back over the years it has become clear how God has used times of suffering and disaster to bring about growth in the church.

After much preparation we launched the appeal in two stages. First we challenged ourselves on the PCC to pledge. If we managed to raise 10 per cent of the budget we would go to the next stage. There was a time of prayer – and the pledges came in. Then we went to the whole church; again we set ourselves a test. By now the budget sum was £275,000. If over £200,000 was pledged by the church we would go ahead and trust that the rest would come in as we built. We had 24 hours of prayer and the sums pledged topped the £200,000 mark. The architect and the builders were bemused that we were depending on pledges rather than money in the bank and that we did not have enough yet to complete the project but, to our relief, they agreed we could start. There was some confusion about whether VAT would be payable on the new building, and the city council at first insisted that it would. But a dogged church member produced an expert opinion from elsewhere and we were saved some extra scores of thousands of pounds.

In the event the extension was completed on time and within budget. It was also beautifully designed and matched the church building. As soon as we opened, it was fully used on Sundays and a new church office opened in the mornings. At last we had space for our administrator to plan her systems efficiently. We did not, however, rush into taking mid-week bookings, because our church hall was already booked out with community use. We wanted the extension to be used strategically, and so reserved some time for prayer and listening to God about possible ways of using this new resource wisely.

There were several other positive results from the new building. Financially we discovered that, though we had been stretched during the six years of the project and some things had been neglected, a whole new generation of people had learned to tithe, and they continued after the building was paid for, enabling us to give more away and to embark on other projects. For many people their involvement in direct giving led them to spiritual growth, which far outstripped the growth in buildings. Our faith muscles were stretched. When renewal came to many parts of the country the next year we had space to accommodate the accompanying growth. We were able to build prayer teams who prayed before the services for the worship and afterwards with people who requested prayer. There were several new babies to take advantage of the new crèche space. The 18s to 25s group, which had hovered round a dozen students for some years, grew under its gifted leaders to over 100, including many who were not students, and moved to the new Upper Room. We were able to have proper supper parties for Alpha and some good social events, so our evangelism could be more in tune with modern needs. Many people in the locality saw that something was happening in the church and came to see. God is always greater than our dreams and within three years of completing the project we were already having to think about another morning service to make room for the new growth.

SACRED AND SECULAR

Several times during our building project we gave thanks that our church building was relatively new and cost little to maintain. Buildings are not always an asset, however. The problem is often at its sharpest in rural areas where small worshipping communities cannot sustain the expense of continually repairing medieval stone church buildings. A radical new approach is going to be needed to break the stalemate between the preservationists and the worshippers. Preservationists want church buildings to be kept as the Victorians left them, but without investing the faith, energy and finance that the Victorians provided to update and restore the ecclesiastical building stock of the land. Worshipping communities would like to keep the church in their village open, but worry that their stewardship of the building is taking up all the time and energy of the church so that none is left for the primary purpose of proclaiming and modelling the kingdom.

In some ways the Victorians by the very success of their Gothic revival are themselves to blame for our present dilemma. It seemed a good idea at the time to open up the chancels and tear down the three-decker pulpits of the eighteenth century; but to put robed choirs and organs in the chancels instead of the monks and priests of medieval times and to disband the village singers and orchestras in the west galleries proved a mixed blessing for their successors.

Now we have to look again at the way we use our village churches. In medieval times the Romney Marsh churches, for instance, were not only used as the village market and school; they were also available for keeping sheep warm during severe parts of the winter. Altar rails were introduced not so much for us to kneel along but to stop the dogs from lifting their legs against the altar! In other words the church building was also the chief community space for the village, and secular and sacred happily coincided, at least in the nave.

The Victorians, by contrast, built church halls for secular use, put costly hangings in the churches, reserving them for sacred use, and filled any remaining nave space with pews. The inevitable result of this unfortunate split into sacred and secular, 150 years later, is that many church buildings can be used only on Sunday mornings, and for six and a half days a week they remain unused and unheated.

Where in a few villages the threat of redundancy has forced the preservationists to allow the removal of pews and the carpeting of the nave, a whole new community space has been created for activities during the week that help to pay for the upkeep of the building. I know of one village church where storage heaters left switched on during the week have enabled regular weekday community and church use of the building. There are problems in multi-purpose use but these are outweighed by the fact that buildings which are well used during the week by the community are much easier to fill on Sundays. The relationship between sacred and secular is also much healthier when the same space is used for blood donation, toddler groups or by-elections during the week as for services on Sunday.

The key questions for churches to ask themselves over the next decade are:

- What buildings will the Church need in this place for its mission?
- Can we usefully share our buildings with other denominations?
- Are our present buildings an asset to the mission of the Church or a millstone round the necks of this and future generations?

Then there will have to be some radical decisions. The Holy Spirit does not ask us to manage decline, but to pray and plan for growth. If we begin with the needs of the population to hear about and experience the love of God in Christ, then decisions about buildings fall into their proper place. It may be difficult to persuade planners that not every Victorian building is a unique part of the national heritage. But this should not prevent us from closing down a few and from erecting the new buildings our generation needs, with the same energy that the Victorians did in their day. The Spirit is calling us to be more than curators of ancient monuments. Where church members are taught to give away a tenth or a tithe of their income they can rise to the challenge of producing the right buildings for the present and the future. God gives his Church in every generation the resources it needs to respond to his goodness.

10
The Clerical Profession

ORDAINED TO SERVE

Historically it can no longer be denied that towards the end of the first century there was a church order according to which a group of 'presbyters' was responsible for the leadership and pastoral care of the local communities.

E. Schillebeeckx[1]

Although much is rapidly changing in the Church, the need for gifted and dedicated parish priests to lead the ministry of the whole church in each parish or group of churches is as great as ever.[2] The New Testament is of course clear that a full-time, paid ministry of 'clergy' is not the only pattern. Whether we look at the case of St Paul, who supported his apostolic ministry by making tents and who was proud that he drew no pay from his congregations, or at a modern group of Christians on a new estate who found a church by starting cell groups, we can see that God's Church is not dependent upon a paid profession. Nevertheless the New Testament is equally clear that Jesus called some disciples to a full-time, dedicated ministry and that it was right for them to be paid, because 'the labourer is worthy of his hire'. The apostolic ministry is the ordered pattern of servicing the Church that has been handed down to us by the Spirit since New Testament times.

In a church in Portovecchia on the island of Corsica there is a prominent stained-glass window, which pictures a large bishop, blessing the islanders; the caption is the famous tag, 'Where the bishop is, there is the Church.'[3] These chapters have argued strongly against a caste of people set aside to be a hierarchy, without which the Church cannot exist or function. Against the popular tag must be set the words of the Lord, 'Where two or three are gathered together in my name, there am I in the midst of them.'[4]

The Church of Christ is necessarily a bottom-up, organic, serving organization, because it is incarnational. It cannot be top-down, dominating, lording it over – without betraying its master.

But nothing in these pages should be taken to say that an every member ministry means that the parochial clergy are unnecessary. Quite the contrary! The more that many and varied ministries bubble up in the local church the greater will be the need to affirm parish priests as God's best pattern both to support the local church and to encourage it to move out into fresh pastures. The more that new ways of being church develop (cell churches, emerging generation churches, church plants, refugee and other special interest congregations), the more obvious it will become that an ordered ministry of wise and experienced pastor-teachers is one of the keys to enabling them to flourish.

MALE AND FEMALE HE CREATED THEM

Leadership in the Old and New Testaments and throughout the history of the Church has been so clearly and unequivocally male that many people wonder how any part of a church could have changed its mind and decided to ordain women – unless through the influence of the secular spirit of this age.

The curious answer to their question is that the arguments for male leadership have simply overreached themselves. On the Catholic side it seems at first sight true that bishops, priests and deacons have been always and exclusively male. But the leap from the kinds of ministry described in the New Testament to that of the classic threefold order of the second- and third-century church fathers is already so great as to build in the concepts of change and development at the heart of Catholic order. And, embarrassingly, women keep popping up in the history of pioneer ministry, doing the apostolic work until it can be routinized by men in the second generation. Catholic order demands that an important change like the ordination of women should be made carefully and reflectively, not that it cannot happen. The 'ecumenical argument', which says that the Church of England has no authority to introduce a novelty like the ordination of women without waiting

for Rome and Orthodoxy, is also superficial. Rome has fo\
unable to recognize our male ministry or (almost) to allow
clergy to marry.

On the Protestant side the very New Testament texts that
so unambiguous overreach themselves if taken at face value. If
women are not to teach or take authority over men but to keep
their heads covered and remain silent, we find ourselves in an
impossible situation. I well remember a highly intelligent and
well-educated woman refusing to sign for taking delivery of a new
carpet because, she said, this would be usurping her husband's
authority! In fact of course these issues were thoroughly explored
at the Reformation; they had to be when Elizabeth became queen
of a Protestant nation and governor of a reformed Church. We
cannot pretend that that work has not been done and go back to a
time where women are not permitted to have any authority over
any men under any circumstances. Nor can a convenient split
between Church and nation or home and society be allowed to
creep in at this point in the argument. The Christian family is still
the right building block for society and the Church is the kingdom
model for the nation.

The texts themselves are more nuanced than some conservative
commentators admit and will not permit themselves to be squeezed
into justifying any traditional church order, whether Presbyterian,
Lutheran, Baptist or Anglican. Ephesians 5.25 is so radically anti-
hierarchical and anti-domination of any kind that it immediately
recalls John 13. The qualifications for leadership are willingness to
embrace sacrifice, humiliation, submission. Any pressing of this
central text would lead to deep male shame.

We have not yet solved all the theological problems raised by
the ordination of women, and must continue to respect those who
cannot agree with it, but the Holy Spirit has moved us forward
to the point where we are no longer at home with the traditional
patterns because we see that they are compatible neither with the
word of God nor the history of the Church. It took 400 years for
the Church to produce theological formulae that matched the
experience of God as Father, Son and Holy Spirit. It may take
more than a generation to produce a theology to match the leading

of the Spirit in our own day that the image of God is both male and female and that in church leadership as in other spheres we belong together.

I have worked both in places where 'leadership is male' was the watchword and also in places where I had to work with a female colleague. Both were highly instructive. It was good to try to take the New Testament seriously and literally about women keeping silent in church and not teaching or having any authority over men, but in practice it led to impossible contradictions; I am convinced now that the teaching of Paul was pointing fundamentally towards the equal worth and partnership of male and female and that his restrictions are wise concessive clauses to avoid scandal in the particular mixed cultural situations of his congregations.

It was also good to work alongside a gifted and experienced Church Army officer (Sister Helen Foster) who had not only been a pioneer evangelist herself but had trained many other Church Army officers before taking early retirement and joining a parish team with a newly appointed and very green priest-in-charge. If she had been a man she would have been a bishop. But the category 'bishop' did not quite fit her – our model is too male. She was nearer Christ in her ministry than most bishops I have known. One day the Church will catch up with women like her.

THE CALL

A fall from over 700 recommended candidates for ordination to the full-time presbyteral ministry in the mid-twentieth century to a little over 200 at the beginning of the twenty-first seems at first sight a disaster for the Church of England. In fact a longer timescale shows more complex fluctuations and other 'low points', which have been the prelude to revivals of faith.[5] The discouraging figures are also tempered by a rise in the number of non-stipendiary ministers, ordained local ministers, Readers and many others, which have transformed our ideas about ministry. There was a substantial rise in the overall number of candidates recommended for ordained ministry in the Decade of Evangelism and after the 1994 Toronto renewal: from around 350 to over 500. More important has been the explosion of lay ministries in our generation, the main effect of which is still to come. If one looks at 'ministries' as opposed to 'vicars', a very different picture of the last 50 years emerges. Nevertheless the decline in the numbers of traditional parochial clergy is real enough and needs to be faced.

What are the factors leading to this decline? They are fairly obvious.

1 Social and political change affecting all institutions and organizations; in general the churches have held up better than all other community groups.
2 Unadventurous and uninspiring modelling, particularly for young people; we have been better at managing advisory boards than calling new ministers.
3 Uncertain theologies of recruitment. For a generation we told younger candidates to go away and find a proper job until they matured – and they did not return.
4 Uneven care during the selection and training process for those who do offer themselves.

Once the decline has been examined it can be tackled and, by God's grace, the tide can be turned. The stories of people who have been called to the ordained ministry reveal that there is a human side to most of them that is not wholly exceptional. God ignites a call in the lives of those who have been influenced and inspired by others, usually a series of contacts: friends, family, fellow students and clergy. It is far from impossible to imagine a Church with rising numbers of ordinands; in fact it is already happening in many parts of the country. But first we need to recover a proper theology of calling in all its richness.

What is the New Testament approach to vocation? In the Gospels the great new commandment is to love as Jesus has loved. It is out of love for the world that his recruitment policy is born.[6] This love is more closely defined in John's Gospel as to 'lay down one's life for one's friends'.[7] The word 'to lay down/lay aside' has the same root as the one that Jesus uses three verses later 'to appoint/ordain' his disciples, to set them aside for their ministry.

The theology of calling here is that God's love is like a vine yielding grapes. It produces friendship and ministry, which produce more sacrificial love, which in turn produces more ministry. A similar confidence – that ministry is a fruit of the Church simply being the Church – infuses all the New Testament documents.

Whenever we say, 'The Lord is here – his Spirit is with us', we are daring to affirm our belief that the risen Jesus is among his people not only to nourish our faith but also to distribute ministry gifts. Ephesians 4 describes how the one Spirit, in obedience to the ascended Christ, produces an explosion of complementary ministries, which work together in harmony.

The decline in ordinations is in part a symptom of a dysfunctional church where the ordained ministry is the only valued calling. However, when many ministries are expected, the cycle of decline becomes a cycle of growth, and congregations become accustomed to seeing people called and equipped. Some of them will be called to ordination. In John 15 the vine responds to being hacked about by producing vigorous new growth; in Ephesians the cross produces a church that, 'when each part is working properly, makes bodily growth and upbuilds itself in love'.

Clergy, it is sometimes said, fear that encouraging lay leadership detracts from their own role. The opposite is rather the case. Where parish priests share their ministry and call many into discipleship and ministry there is growth such that their leadership is stretched and in greater demand. It has also been said that the real ministry of the laity is out in the world and not in the sanctuary. This is to misunderstand the relationship between the two. Properly understood, lay ministries in church enhance, prepare for and model ministries in the marketplace. While there are different balances to be drawn in all our lives, a healthy missionary church serving the world is dependent upon most church members discovering their gifting and ministries. Just as it took many years for the threefold ministry to emerge from all the ministries mentioned in the New Testament, so ordained ministries take time to nurture from among the wealth of ministries in the modern congregation. 'It is in the formation of Christian communities that particular gifts for ministry will be recognised.'[8] In other words if we want more ministers, lay and ordained, then we should expect to be involved in more mission, evangelism, discipling, formation and patient Christian community-building after the model of Jesus and the apostles.

A useful parallel is that of stewardship. A generation ago Anglicans expected to be subsidized by money from the past. No one quite knew where the money came from or why it was being used for maintenance rather than mission, but we accepted it as a kind of 'given'. Some even tried to justify it. Since then we have come to see that our lack of proportional giving out of present income is a symptom of a deeper spiritual malaise; and in very few years great strides have been made to change us from a subsidized Church towards being an interdependent and sharing Church.

Similarly the average congregation has not been encouraged to ask where vicars come from. They were a 'given'. But recently the (unknown) source seems to have dried up. Just as we now believe that God has given to his people all the financial resources we need to be an effective Church, so we are called at the beginning of a new century to believe that he has given us all the gifted people we need to be the Church for the world. There may be good reason why in a particular place or time there should be shortage, but on the whole *ubi caritas ibi diakonia.*[9] It would be very odd if we were to find ourselves saying in effect that there are not enough suitable people in our nation for the ordained ministry of the Church.

The task of the next decade is to 'pray the Lord of the harvest to call out labourers into his harvest'. Our part in this will be to give to our congregations a fresh vision that it can happen, and that it is normal church life to expect it; then to model the process helpfully, to remove the stumbling blocks, and to sharpen up our formation of ministers. As in the case of stewardship there is much that we can learn from other parts of the Anglican Communion about how people are recruited to the priesthood.

Here are a few practical suggestions for churches.

1 *Prayer.* A vocations policy could easily become a merely secular management exercise without a foundation of waiting upon God for a specific vision.
2 *Deciding needs.* It should be possible to calculate how many people are needed

- to maintain a diocesan strength;
- to make a proper contribution to the national pool;
- to second a proportion to mission work overseas.

Then the bishops can make this target known for prayer.

3 *Congregational calling.* We should encourage the trend for congregations to discern those among them who have special gifts and calling.

4 *Care of ordinands.* Congregations have plenty of opportunity to observe the quality of care and training that ordinands receive. It is a factor in encouraging or discouraging others to offer themselves.

5 *Cycle of training.* Work can be done on the whole cycle of pre-ordination, post-ordination and continuing ministerial formation. Why are there drop-outs and are there things to be learned?

6 *Parochial training.* Is there a place for more parochially based, on-the-job training for those would-be non-stipendiary ministers who are already competent and articulate in their faith and who because of their gifts are in demanding jobs?

7 *The new churches.* We can learn from the new churches why and how they call so many young people into leadership.

8 *Youth.* The statistics indicate that 'the recent drop in numbers coming forward for ordained ministry is almost wholly represented by a drop in candidates in the 20–30 age range'.[10] Considering how few young people there have been in our churches over the last few decades it is a wonder that the drop in numbers has not happened sooner. There is much to be done in implementing the *Youth A Part* Report (1996)[11] with its recommendations on allowing young people to discover and use ministry gifts. We cannot afford a Church that ignores young people. Dioceses and regions could run annual vocations conferences for older pupils with top-class national speakers.

9 *Work experience.* I have had good experience of welcoming work-experience students from schools, but so far the initiative has come from the schools rather than from the churches.

10 *Youth ministers.* Many of our youth workers are the age
    that curates used to be. They are an increasingly useful
    resource in their own right and a vital connection with
    youth culture. Because youth are best at evangelizing their
    own generation, there is much that a vocations panel could
    learn from them.

For a church to work effectively, it must be seen as a school for
discipleship, where the formation of leaders, lay and ordained, and
the modelling of how ministers and priests are called, equipped
and sustained are a key part of being a church. The Holy Spirit has
not withdrawn his ministry gifts from our churches. We have in
our generation a fresh opportunity to see the church 'upbuilding
itself in love'.

The calling to ordained ministry does not happen in a vacuum.
It is one of the fruits of a church where all are being helped from
a young age to discover how they can contribute to the kingdom. I
am delighted that young people from our parish are courageously
serving God in many different parts of the world and being
supported by those who have stayed in this country.

TRAINING THE TRAINERS

It is Wednesday night and the first evening of the new term at the
South-East Institute of Theology at Canterbury. The 12 students
are starting their New Testament course. Most of them are still
blissfully unaware of the difference between structural and redac-
tion criticism or eschatology and apocalyptic, but all know that
handling the Bible will be a key to their new lives. The six women
and six men vary in age from 35 to 59 and come with a variety of
Christian and work experience. They are preparing for ordained
ministry in the Church of England by studying part-time for three
years while maintaining their present jobs.

At present there are 12 theological colleges and 12 regional
theological courses in England and Wales. The question raised by
many who have come through the traditional theological college
system about the courses is whether it is possible to educate the
clergy part-time or whether this leads to a lowering of standards

to an extent that will damage the Church.[12] This may well be the wrong question, based on the premise that initial training is all we need to set us up as qualified clergy. If the clergy are called to model a life of discipleship and ministry formation, however, the initial period looks rather different. The church has been offered a dazzling variety of gifts and talents by its mature ordinands over the past 30 years. It has not always known how to accept these people properly. In particular it has not found it easy to use their experience in the training period. Young staff on the training courses often find themselves faced with people who are more mature as Christians, have more experience of church life and who have a wide range of gifts. If they simply deliver a cut-down version of their own experience of a theological college, if they have little knowledge of adult education, results can be disappointing.

It is still rare for there to be much pastoral and missionary experience in some places. It would be strange to go through medical school without being trained by those with experience as doctors, but it is common to go through a theological college or course where only the tutor in pastoral studies has been an incumbent. Perhaps a helpful model is the old teacher-training colleges, where some of the staff were experts in an academic discipline and others were experienced and reflective teachers. It was in the interaction of the two types of expert that a good formation was made possible. Ordinands need stretching both in their academic studies and in pastoral and missionary experience. The formation of presbyters cannot be left to a single four-year curacy.

One of the success stories of the recent past has been the move of the Church Army Training College to Sheffield and the location of the Association of Church Planting at the Sheffield Centre. Here we have an increasingly confident training of evangelists for church planting or youth and community work all over the country and especially in the north. The courses and colleges might learn from the way that Church Army links theory and practice in their college.

PAY AND CONDITIONS

Another weakness in the care and nurture of our leaders has been the neglect of a proper employment package that can stand up to modern scrutiny. There has been an extraordinary unwillingness on the part of the English churches to face up to their obligations towards paying their clergy fairly. It has been matched by an almost equal unwillingness on the part of the clergy to give up the freehold in exchange for proper conditions of service.

In common with most other clergy of our generation we spent our early years after ordination on Family Income Supplement. The Church had shuffled off some of its responsibilities towards its curates on to the state. It also hid behind a confusion about the difference between a 'stipend' and a 'wage', or between a 'calling' and a 'job'. This is a confusion because, as Anthony Russell pointed out long ago, the two are simply different ways of looking at the same thing.[13] A 'calling' and a 'stipend' look at the ministry from a theological point of view; a 'wage' and a 'job' look at it from a sociological point of view. Neither can be excluded, and to confuse the two is disgraceful. It was common to argue that parochial clergy should be paid modest stipends for theological reasons, but bishops and other senior clergy should be paid large salaries for sociological reasons. The traditional criterion, that Anglican clergy are paid not a wage but a stipend just large enough to enable them and their family to live free of financial anxiety, is here ignored.

Some years ago it was pointed out that the long-accepted principle that we pay incumbents just enough to enable them live without undue anxiety meant that the Church was deliberately paying assistant clergy below that minimum level. There was some worrying evidence that people competent enough to do the sums have been unwilling to put this undue pressure on their families and withdrawn their applications, leaving us with a higher than healthy proportion of clergy who cannot manage finances. A pragmatic solution has been to bring assistant clergy pay almost up to a level with that of incumbents, thus flattening out the differentials of over 90 per cent of our employees. Not surprisingly this has not been good for the morale of experienced clergy.

In fact differentials in pay are a just and proper way of valuing different levels of responsibility and sacrifice of privacy. The Church of England should be modelling to the nation how a fair differentials policy would work. But the excessive differentials between vicars and bishops are not justifiable and this problem is not properly addressed in Richard Turnbull's otherwise useful report.[14] The stipend of an incumbent after ten years of service needs to be raised some 25 to 30 per cent to increase the differentials with assistant staff and to decrease them with senior clergy.

The question many will ask is whether or not the Church could afford a properly paid clergy. It has already answered that question when it comes to the other professionals whom it employs. Good people are worth their hire. Good parish priests soon pay for themselves. In fact we cannot afford not to provide properly for our clergy. Clergy, like other Christians, are called to live modestly, to embrace poverty. But it must be voluntary poverty, not an excuse for evading our responsibilities as employer.

Most clergy have put their energies elsewhere than concerning themselves about pay and conditions. But the anomalies have sometimes seriously hampered the well-being of their dependants. A proper, caring package of pay and conditions, including small differentials, and a means for saving up for retirement housing, needs to be introduced. It would offer better protection than the outdated freehold and could be a helpful model for other large organizations.

APPRAISAL FOR GROWTH

> *Do not be like a horse or a mule without understanding, whose temper must be curbed with bit and bridle, else it will not stay near you.*

> (Psalm 32.9, NRSV)

In most professions today fundamental changes are being brought about by appraisal and in-service training. GPs are being helped by extensive video training to improve the way in which they approach patients. With the right encouragement it would be possible to help clergy in some of our skills too. Until recently most church leaders have lived and worked in splendid isolation, accountable to no one except our own vision of God. The lack of appraisal may protect our self-esteem in the short term but denies us that chance to grow which good appraisal allows.

Adults do not disciple easily. For new learning to take plac
an adult who is in mid-career and used to having his or her o
way at the workplace, a certain amount of challenge and even
unlearning has to take place before the new learning can take place.
Jesus was well aware of this problem, which is why he so often
scandalized his adult hearers. There usually has to be a 'disclosure
situation' or a 'paradigm shift' in which one is suddenly aware that
one is being summoned to change.[15] The lawyer in Luke 10.25 asks
Jesus about eternal life and who his neighbour is, and finds himself (in his imagination) not, as he expected, handing out largesse
to the deserving poor from his comfortable position but wounded
and desperate to receive help, abandoned by his colleagues who
pass by on the other side, and unable to protest when a despised
outsider pays for unlimited care for him. This is a learning situation, par excellence!

The most appropriate biblical and theological word for such
ongoing learning is repentance, *metanoia*, 'a new mind': 'Be transformed by the renewal of your mind, that you may prove what is
the will of God . . . good and acceptable and perfect.'[16] Every day
Christians examine themselves before God, confess their sins,
receive forgiveness and ask for the help of the Holy Spirit to
amend their lives. This is the spiritual and liturgical foundation
for appraisal: self-appraisal and appraisal by God.

Just as prayer in private is foundational but not sufficient for a
fruitful spiritual life, so the private *examen de conscience* is not
sufficient appraisal for ongoing growth in discipleship. One of the
reasons for depression among clergy and church leaders is that we
know deep down that we are holding our people back because we
have become stuck somewhere in our discipleship, but we do not
know quite where or exactly what to do about it. Development in
different areas is important for church leaders. Appraisal in each of
these areas can be seen at first as a threat and as unkind criticism,
but with perseverance it can become a great release as skills and
working relationships improve. In most denominations there has
been a recognition that appraisal is important and a spate of
schemes has been introduced.[17]

Most clergy are grateful that some interest is being shown in
them and in the intractable problems they face, and the current

appraisal systems are usually geared to encouraging and affirming the front-line troops. The problem with present appraisal schemes is that they are not nearly thorough enough. No one has ever sat and listened to me preach or assessed my interviewing skills or chairmanship or how I lead worship. The fundamental issues with the clergy are these: If I am not under effective authority myself, how can I exercise it with others? If I am not learning to climb out of my various ruts in mid-life, how can I show others how to get out of theirs? If we are not producing a new generation of young leaders, is it because of arrested development in our discipleship and learning? 'The truth will set you free' is not an abstract concept but a key part of Christian growth.[18]

For appraisal to work it has to be carried on at several different levels. First is self-assessment, which is one of the classical spiritual disciplines that can be extended to cover ministry skills. Some dioceses send out checklists, which can be worked through in private. Second is the appraisal that a good lay team can offer. I have benefited enormously from the wise comments offered by supportive colleagues over the years. Third comes peer review – a great antidote to the common situation where fellow church leaders are often virtual strangers or even competitors. Unity is prevented as much by lack of proper structures for working together as by doctrinal differences. Fourth comes pastoral appraisal by the bishop or other officer. My own diocese has been actively developing this kind of warm and affirmative appraisal; it demands some sacrifice of time by already busy senior church leaders but is appreciated by the clergy. Fifth is appraisal by consultants in specialist areas who can help with particular skills or spiritual development.

Sixth is the line manager, who is there to ask sharp but not unfriendly questions about the overall direction of one's ministry and the balancing of priorities and skills. I experienced this recently when a new archdeacon took over a department, including a diocesan committee that I chair. He asked me to go and see him and quizzed me about the committee: What was my aim as chairman? How did I monitor progress? Were the various bishop's officers achieving their potential? Had the recent archbishop's missions really been worth the trouble? and so on. I came back from the interview brimming with fresh ideas. Those who say that bishops and archdeacons are in danger of becoming business managers rather than spiritual leaders ignore how pastoral it can be to have a spiritually minded line manager. But as in any other kind of learning the initial enthusiasm for change needs to be followed up and monitored. An appraisal that is not followed up, progress that is not monitored and encouraged, can lead to despair.

The main Old Testament model of redemption is the liberation of the people of Israel from bondage in Egypt. The New Testament takes this up with a new stress on internal loosing of shackles and the liberty of the Spirit. The new liberty brings with it a new responsibility. It has to be recognized from the outset that the proper independence of the clergy means that ministers are each responsible for enabling their own appraisal as they are for finding their own spiritual director. Leaders in the local church are painfully aware of their own shortcomings that prevent growth. The Holy Spirit brings an initial experience of release, and a new determination to make repentance ongoing in every area of ministry. A multifaceted and flexible system of appraisals is an important part of responding to the work of the Spirit.

LINE MANAGEMENT

When people have worked in an episcopal system they usually come to value it. To be able to say, 'I am under authority' and to have to practise obedience is countercultural and against the snake.[19] To be commissioned by a wise pastor who may say, 'I want you to shake this parish up. They won't like it, because they are too comfortable, but I want you to do it' is a stretching and fulfilling thing. And when there are problems in a local church it is good to have someone over one with a more objective eye. I am in favour of bishops for practical as well as historical and theological reasons. Every front-line pastor needs someone standing behind him or her.

But sometimes it seems as if the bishops are caught in a web, which frustrates them and the Church which they long to serve. They are usually too busy; they have too many responsibilities to be chief pastor and an effective leader of mission, teacher of the faith and the other things which they are appointed to be; and sometimes they are driven to the brink of exhaustion by the weight of it all. The structure of huge dioceses goes back to Augustine's mission to the Anglo-Saxons and the reorganization of the church by his successor Theodore. Pope Gregory, who sent Augustine and his monks to Britain, wrote a book called *The Book of the Pastoral Rule*[20] in which the assumption was that the bishop was the chief pastor of a small city. In his experience in Southern Italy, cities were densely packed, so there were large numbers of bishops.[21] Even so Gregory made two demands on each of his bishops that discouraged the enlarging of dioceses: first, that he keep a close eye on the health of his people; and second, that he keep himself humble as a leader. Theodore of Tarsus (602–90 AD) came to be Archbishop of Canterbury from Asia Minor where cities and bishops were equally densely packed and his principle was 'That more bishops be created as the number of faithful increases'.[22] In other words the principle on which both Gregory and Theodore built their mission was that the church leaders should lead the church by serving it, not the other way round. This was the way to spiritual health both for the churches and for the bishops.

But Anglo-Saxon England, like Gaul, was resistant to this part of the gospel. For one thing the cities were far more widely dispersed than in Southern Europe and Asia Minor. For another bishops were usually of noble birth and were expected to have the lifestyle of the nobility. To maintain such a lifestyle demanded large dioceses with substantial income. According to Bede, the Anglo-Saxon bishops resisted their archbishop in his desire to have more bishops and smaller dioceses. The result was dioceses based on kingdoms rather than on congregations. This is why Canterbury rather than London became the seat of the archbishop, because Kent dominated Essex.

In recent years there was an opportunity to create a small diocese, still larger than that expected by Gregory or Theodore, but more workable than most present English dioceses. Croydon was a compact archdeaconry in the diocese of Canterbury but separated from it for obscure historical reasons. The experience of those who

worked as parish priests in Croydon was quite different from elsewhere; they regarded the area bishop as a personal friend, who
knew them well, and area meetings were intimate and purposeful.
Somehow the opportunity to have an experimental small urban
diocese in England was missed and Croydon has become part of
Southwark, now one of the largest and least manageable of our
great urban dioceses. The reasons for not leaving Croydon on its
own had, as usual, to do with administration, the needs of clergy
job satisfaction and episcopal status, rather than the mission of the
church at local level. Once again the Anglo–Saxon approach won
over the gospel!

Another way ahead, which will be increasingly tried over the
next few years, is to make rural deans into a kind of suffragan
bishop. Of course history cannot be ignored, and there is much in
our history to be valued, but if Christians, including bishops, are
to be properly nourished then thought will be given in each
generation to units of pastoral care that make for health and
growth. Jesus chose 12 men and all the research shows that groups
somewhere between eight and 15 are the natural size for someone
to pastor. As Rural Dean I found that ten parishes made a workable unit, but when the non-parochial clergy were included, 18
were really too many for a busy vicar to pastor and I did not do it
effectively. I understood why the old Latin title for my office,
Decanus, implies a unit of ten. It seems that effective pastoral care
and nurture, starting from the local Christians, would produce a
system where, in urban areas at least, ten or so 'household units'
would make one house group, ten or so house groups would make
a congregation with one full-time worker, ten or so congregations
would make a deanery, ten or so deaneries a diocese, and ten or so
dioceses a province.[23]

Tradition is important, and it is humbling to see the lists of
bishops in many a diocese going back into the Dark Ages and in
some cases beyond. But tradition does not always serve the gospel,
as Jesus had often to point out to his contemporaries.[24] Those of us
who advocate episcopacy reason that God has provided bishops to
serve the Church. I sometimes wonder, however, if the large ancient
sees really serve a romantic idea about the Church rather than its
mission today. If the tradition of large dioceses is preventing the

people from hearing the gospel then the tradition must be challenged and if necessary new mission structures brought in, which are more in tune with the needs of the gospel.

LIVING WITH STRESS AND FAILURE

They made me keeper of the vineyards,
but my own vineyard I have not kept!
(Song of Songs 1.6, NRSV)

However, there are more pressing problems on local church leaders than the size of dioceses. All professions have become increasingly demanding over the last 25 years. The promise of leisure in a post-industrial society has failed to materialize for most workers. The much discussed 'life/work balance' is elusive. The new partnership between men and women, sharing the delights of home and work, is still problematic. Teachers and health professionals in particular have suffered such demands upon their professions that many are abandoning their calling for the sake of their own health and sanity. They are not alone.

The clergy have not escaped these pressures and have some of their own to add. We are habitually short of time, money and space. People can usually survive relative poverty well if they have physical space and time. They can cope with lack of time if they have some money. But if all three are chronically absent then strains and stresses start to appear. Like local doctors of 50 years ago, clergy work from their homes, and their families become receptionists. I have abiding memories of Jane, with a baby in one arm, a toddler on a bike at her feet, sorting enquirers, keys and shopping simultaneously, like a triage nurse on the Western Front. We counted recently and, including the children's groups on a Sunday morning, discovered that over 250 people passed through our vicarage in a week, some of them while we should have been enjoying family time.

When I first went to Folkestone I asked the Baptist minister, who had taken some interest in me, how he managed the pressures. He told me that if he had his time over again he would spend much more time with his teenage children. I remembered that advice and was therefore all the more devastated when, ten years later, my own children told me that, though I was often at home, they felt I was so absorbed in the work of the church that I had no time to welcome their friends or even to be available to them.

However, the time problem is not the root of the matter. As with other 'emergency services' we are pleased to be ready to be called out at any time for real emergencies. But the temptation to the vicar, as to the old-fashioned local doctor who worked on his own, is to model strength, reassurance and a kind of avuncular, all-encompassing competence. Like the swan, which glides over water while (invisibly) paddling furiously beneath, the leader of a local church is often inwardly in crisis while apparently gliding over circumstances. St Paul, by contrast, boasts of weakness, his vulnerability, his desperation. The second epistle to the Corinthians is a manual for stressed-out leaders. Paul and his companions took on all the sophistication of the Greek cities of his time, knowing that apostles were 'clay pots': brittle, vulnerable, of humble origin. Recently I flew over the barren Toros mountains and thought of St Paul crossing them on foot, 'in toil and hardship, through many a sleepless night, in hunger and thirst, often without food, in cold and exposure. And, apart from other things, there is the daily pressure upon me of my anxiety for all the churches.'[25]

The point which is perhaps most difficult for us to grasp is that St Paul, like Jesus, was not afraid to be against his culture in his understanding of leadership. Christianity overcame, not by winning, but by being endlessly defeated. In that sense, Christianity is a religion of failure. It is this which Nietzsche despised. In our culture too, the preoccupation with success and power is seductive. The danger, particularly for Christians wanting to recover the supernatural dimension of the New Testament, is that miracles and even prayer can become our winning formulae in the game of success.[26] If we succumb to the temptation to chase personal success we will find ourselves travelling in the direction opposite to the apostles. Just as the blood of the martyrs was the seed of the early Church, so apparent defeat and weakness in the modern Church can often be the occasion of greater growth than the miracles and the new buildings, because they can model 'grace' rather than 'works'. The Church is nothing without Pentecost, but Pentecost has not replaced the way of the cross. Though Christ paid for our redemption on the cross and there is nothing left for us to pay, that does not mean we are exempt from its sufferings. In so far as we set up the cross in our hearts we will taste some of the penalties of unconditional love in our own lives. That is the 'divine office' of all Christians, but particularly of those called to church leadership.[27] That does not mean either that we are to be content with second best for our churches or that we can neglect the care of our selves and our families. Christian ministry is more of a marathon than a sprint and we have to be nourished and sustained for the long haul if we and those close to us are to survive.

I am grateful to those who have spotted when I have exhausted myself and have encouraged me to adopt the following strategies. They have had to repeat their advice often.

- Failure and vulnerability are built into being fully human and are to be embraced;
- isolation in leadership is to be shunned; we are made to work in teams and, in the case of ministers, in chapters and ministers' meetings as a first priority;
- we can only move forward if we spend time in retreat;
- no one is a real person without hobbies and interests outside the church;
- family and friends are a gift to be treasured. Single clergy in particular need to be given time to travel and spend with friends;
- only a home that is first closed and private can be opened to others. An open home is not the same as a railway station;
- God has put us under human as well as divine authority for our own good so that we do not worry above our station;
- the spiritual life goes in seasons and rhythms. The dark night of the soul comes round as regularly as the personal Pentecost;
- it is better to love extravagantly than to win battles.

The last word on this subject, however, must go to George Herbert:

Pitch thy behaviour low, thy projects high;
So shalt thou humble and magnanimous be.
Sink not in spirit: Who aimeth at the sky,
Shoots higher much than he that means a tree.
　　A grain of glory mixt with humbleness
　　Cures both a fever and lethargicness.[28]

11
Being a Pastor

PASTORAL CARE

The first service that one owes to others is listening to them. Just as love of God begins with listening to His word, so the beginning of love for the brethren is learning to listen to them.
Dietrich Bonhoeffer[1]

One of the great gifts that the Christian Church has given to the world, only dimly reflected in the modern concept of human rights, is the belief that we are loved and cared for by God and that therefore each of us, however flawed, is infinitely precious and worth listening to. Pastoral care starts in the nature of God, who reveals himself in the Scriptures as carer, helpmate, mother hen, lover, husband, father and shepherd.

In the Old Testament Yahweh is the shepherd of Israel and chief pastor of the flock. Ezekiel 34 is the key passage that makes clear what pastoral care is not. The prophet indignantly protests to the shepherd/leaders of Israel about their exploitation of those whom they should have served.[2] Pastoral care, according to this passage, involves searching out and seeking for the lost – mission and pastoral care cannot ultimately be divided. It involves binding up the wounds and making strong again. It includes a watching over the strong and healthy, rather than simply assuming that those who are not causing trouble are fit and well, and a strong sense of justice on behalf of the have-nots. This is a rich seam to mine. It is worth comparing with Psalm 23, which speaks of a personal relationship with the Shepherd who leads and guides, who accompanies his flock through danger and death and who finally brings his flock to dwell in his own house for ever.

It is against this background that Jesus calls himself the Good Shepherd and adds to the Old Testament account the securing of eternal life and salvation from sin, the laying down of his life for the sheep, the intimate knowledge of and friendship with them and the mission to other flocks and folds.[3] The parable of the Good Samaritan fills out this job description with the picture of healing and tender care; the Hebrew/Aramaic for Samaritan and watchman/shepherd are too close for St Luke to have missed the connection.[4]

An important part of the training of the apostles by Jesus is to help them understand that leadership and pastoral care are to be learned from the love of God. St John in particular emphasizes that Jesus sees his task as making known the character of God to his disciples so that the love of the Father for the Son may be in them – a hugely ambitious aim: 'I made your name known to them, and I will make it known, so that the love with which you have loved me may be in them, and I in them.'[5]

Pastoral care, in other words, is the transfer of a powerful, caring love from the *koinonia* of the Trinitarian God to his people. So the risen Jesus commissions Peter to tend his sheep by pushing him hard: not on how well he has learned techniques of pastoral care, but on the extent and quality of his love. Equally the quality of the leader's love for God is manifested by the quality of true pastoral care that he will provide.[6] In turn, and much later in his life, the apostle will call on his fellow elders to:

> Tend the flock of God that is your charge, not by constraint but willingly, not for shameful gain but eagerly, not as domineering over those in your charge but being examples to the flock. And when the chief Shepherd is manifested you will obtain the unfading crown of glory.[7]

Most local congregations understand this well, and most clergy and Readers in particular give themselves heroically to loving their flocks. If you investigate what holds churches together when the worship and the preaching are less than inspiring it often turns out to be the quality of care that a congregation provides for its members. Church members will forgive their pastors most things if they have been on the receiving end of real pastoral care at a time of crisis in their own lives.

However, the amount of pastoral care that a congregation can demand from its leaders is potentially infinite. One of the most wearing aspects of the pastoral ministry is being on duty 24 hours a day. People often die in the small hours, crises often arise when the parish priest is just settling down with his own family for a birthday, and the first visit always seems to open up the need for a second and third. Sometimes it is good that sermon preparation is interrupted by an urgent call but if, over the years, the standard of preaching is permanently lowered by the pressure of pastoral need, then clearly a whole congregation is in danger of being weakened.

As a result, most of us parish priests labour under a burden of guilt. There is always someone we promised to visit and have not, always a family member we have not spent time with, always a task left undone. It is cheering to read that John Chrysostom in the fourth century experienced the same pressure and that 'he did not visit me' was a cry of reproach in his day.[8] Even longer ago, Moses, who was also known as the pastor of Israel, suffered from too many people to care for, and a wise member of his family observed that what he needed if he was going to care effectively for his demanding flock was a system.[9]

Pastors who allow themselves to be seduced by the idea that they must provide all the pastoral care drive themselves into an early grave and prevent a congregation from growing larger. Jethro's word to Moses could well be a word to many of our churches: 'You and the people with you will wear yourselves out.' God is our model for the quality of pastoral care we show, but he cannot be the model for the quantity. One of the key expectations of both Old and New Testaments is that those responsible for pastoral care are teachers. They listen to God and receive from him before they teach his word. The call of Ezekiel, for instance, begins with a revelation of the majesty and strangeness of the Godhead. As part of this vision the prophet is shown a written scroll and commanded to eat it. 'Then I ate it; and it was in my mouth as sweet as honey.'[10] No one can adequately care for the flock of Israel without having ingested the word of God in such a way that it can be taught and proclaimed. A key part of pastoring therefore is teaching.

Jesus himself cared for his little flock by constantly teaching them about the kingdom. This is also the implication of the Lord's word to Peter, 'Feed my lambs';[11] and the pastor as teacher is the primary New Testament model.[12] So in the epistle to the Hebrews the writer declares that the fact that they do not appear to understand this is a sign that they need clearer basic teaching: 'You need milk, not solid food; for every one who lives on milk, being still an infant, is unskilled in the word of righteousness.'[13]

The aim of pastoral care is not simply to bring comfort and consolation, but to enable people to develop and grow into the kind of people they were created to be:

- first, that change is possible, that the gospel seed will bear fruit in a receptive soil;
- second, that the power of the Holy Spirit is available to help us grow and change;
- and third, that the context within which we grow as Christians is the Church.

St Paul often speaks of this maturing as a process in which the pastor and the believers are partners with the Holy Spirit. In his first letter to the Corinthians, the Christians are a field, the apostles are the agricultural labourers and the Holy Spirit makes them grow.[14] In the second letter to the same church the Christians are God's letter to the world, revealing how God's glorious image is being restored in their lives, and Paul is the delivery boy.[15] In Galatians he is like a woman in labour, yearning to give birth to mature Christians.[16] He longs 'to present every Christian mature in Christ'[17] and says that the work of the ministries of the Church is to enable all to 'grow up in every way into him who is the head'.[18] It is through praying constantly for his people that he is able to encourage and teach them.

When pastoral care in the local church is working properly we grow in grace. Sometimes this can be quite dramatic as the Holy Spirit prompts about a particular character trait or releases us from some old chains that have bound us since childhood; usually it is slow and imperceptible to the individual Christian; and always there is the constant reminder that in this life change is only partial because we carry the great treasure of Christ in earthen vessels. All of us are aware of how far we fall short of what we might be. At times we are all aware of how we disappoint those who have to live and work with us. We all of us hunger for God.

> Everyone is on the verge of crying out, 'My Lord and my God!' but the cry is drowned out by doubts or defiance, muffled by the dull ache of routines, masked by cosy accommodations with mediocrity. Then something happens – a word, an event, a dream – and there is a push towards an awareness of an incredible Grace, a dazzling Desire, a defiant Hope, a courageous Faithfulness. But awareness, as such, is not enough . . . The Pastor is there to nudge the awareness past subjectivities and ideologies and into the open and say 'God.'[19]

PASTORAL VISITING

My first vicar took me visiting with him in the week after my ordination. I still remember some of those visits, in particular the first funeral visit. Mr Jones had been a farmer and we called on a relative, also a farmer, for some details about the deceased. 'So Mr Jones was a popular man hereabouts?' began my vicar brightly. The relative looked at him. ''E were a reet old boogger,' he said sourly.

It is no longer true that a home-visiting parson makes a churchgoing parish. Whole areas are empty and deserted during the afternoons. Blocks of flats are difficult to break into at any time. But home visiting is still an essential part of pastoral ministry. For the parish priest it is a tremendous privilege to knock on doors and know that in most parts of the country you will still be welcomed. However busy the parish there is no substitute for tramping the streets or hedgerows. Gone are the times for most of us when the ordained minister can visit the whole parish, or even the whole congregation. But we can make sure that the whole patch is visited and leafleted regularly, that new people moving in are welcomed, and that everyone knows where their local church is and who the nearest contact people are. A Christmas and Easter card, perhaps printed with services of all the denominations in the area, a welcome leaflet, a sample magazine to distribute one street at a time – these are seeds that will not bear fruit immediately but will make visiting easier.[20]

These days most churches also organize the pastoral visiting of the sick. If people are assigned to housegroups or street wardens it can happen naturally and informally. There are still those who feel that the church has not visited until the vicar has been, but they have to be politely put right, if the lay people are not to be denied an important and fruitful ministry. Visiting with the sacraments those who through age or sickness cannot come to church is a responsibility welcomed by prayerful lay people; there are ten nursing homes in my parish and lay teams visit each one. As a result of her involvement in nursing home services, one of our Readers is increasingly being asked to take the funerals of those she has faithfully visited and her ministry is much valued by the parish.

What is the deeper purpose of visiting? There is not much better advice than that of Richard Baxter who, when he began as Vicar of Kidderminster, found only one churchgoing family in the town, and when he finished had only two not attending. His method, distilled, was to put three questions to those whom he visited: 'What has God done for you recently?' 'What have you done for God?' and 'How can I help?'[21] I have the same questions at the back of my mind as we talk, and find they often produce surprising revelations that lead naturally into prayer. In fact my experience is that evening visiting is far more fruitful than many a church committee meeting. I estimate that if I visit three households in an evening (after a baptism or wedding or funeral request) I would be disappointed if one of them at least did not end up having a regular connection with the church.

THE PASTORAL OFFICES

BAPTISMS

One of the inglorious confusions of church life today is over baptism. There are three distinct theologies of baptism at large today, and many variations. The first, held by the greater proportion of Christendom, states after Augustine that the sacraments are a means of grace, which should not be denied to any who come seeking them. Any fencing about of baptism is, in this view, a denial of the prodigal hospitality of God, and any restricting of the sacrament to those who are capable of answering for themselves is in danger of excluding any who fail an arbitrary intelligence test.

The second, held by the section of the Church that is growing most vigorously today – the Pentecostal, Baptist and New Church Christians – states that it is scandalous to baptize babies who can know nothing of commitment to Christ, that the baptism of whole populations has done nothing for those nations or for the denominations which practise it and that the New Testament expects adult conversion and commitment before baptism, clearly marking out Christians from the general public.

The third view, held by the reformed churches including Anglican evangelicals, is an intermediate one. It holds that the New Testament clearly deals in families and covenants as well as individuals and that it is therefore wrong to bring up the children of believing parents as if they were outside the Church. So baptism is first for converted adults and second for their children.[22]

Like all Anglican ministers I have been through the debates about infant baptism many times over the years and have belonged to churches that have taken mixtures of the first and third view, and that have had several members who have embraced the second. I have also enjoyed the friendship of Baptist ministers who have quietly confessed to being closet paedobaptists.

The pastoral consequences of trying to change from theology One to theology Two/Three would be a nightmare, even if the Church of England could be persuaded to agree to make such a change. It is not the fault of the people of this country that they have been taught for centuries that babies should automatically be baptized soon after birth. A change would be necessary if it became clear that the New Testament demanded it and that, as in some other questions, we had been wrong until now. But my Baptist friends freely admit that the problem of people breaking their vows is not simply a problem for paedobaptists. The chief objection to the second theology, popular though it is, is that it makes baptism more of a witness to the faith of the candidates than to the faithfulness of the Lord. We rightly speak of 'being baptized' in the passive voice, because ultimately being joined to Christ is something that God does to and for us, not something we do as a badge of our faith. A robust biblical case can be made out for the third theological view and for Anglican practice; it takes a little longer to state than the second but is none the worse for that.

The debate, although unresolved, is less pressing than a decade ago, partly because of the fall-off in the number of baptisms. Those parents still asking for baptism are usually serious about it. If the local church responds with equal seriousness these applications provide a big evangelistic opportunity. There are at least three challenges. It is the responsibility of the church family to provide such a welcome that the baptism party feel God's welcome; if our style of worship is alien to the culture of the parish, and if the usual congregation treat the newcomers as intruders, they will not come back. If the arrangements for other children are good so that they meet some friends from school, and if parents and godparents sense that God is real and to be encountered, then they will. The second challenge is the parish's willingness to have convenient introductory courses to the Christian faith and parenting. These days, because of babysitting problems, we often have to go to parents rather than have the preparation course at a central point. The third challenge is to the parish priest and his or her colleagues who have to make some spiritual judgement as to where the parents are in their relationship with God and how therefore to explain the meaning of the vows to them and the godparents in a way that stretches them and leads them on without putting wrong stumbling blocks in their paths.

Twenty years ago I thought it was my main duty to prevent casual enquirers for infant baptism from perjuring themselves and dishonouring God's house. But I believe now that the greater challenge is to the believing community, to show open-handed support to young parents caught up in a world of chaotic and dysfunctional family relationships. Baptism is such an important ceremony that it is a pity to cram it into a gap in the Eucharist. Christian initiation deserves a service that explores some of the implications of becoming disciples of Christ. This is best done in most cases not in the afternoon but in the morning service where the congregation can welcome the family and pledge their support.

We have begun experimenting with the Beatitudes as a kind of response to a baptismal liturgy which, together with exuberant praise, prayer, readings and a sermon, provide more than enough for a rich service of word and sacrament.

More and more children are surviving to their teenage years without being baptized and, if they then come to faith, there is much to celebrate. As teenagers and students do things corporately it is probable that the candidates' friends will also have been baptized recently, as like as not by full immersion in a tank or a swimming pool. While not wanting to give way on the point that the amount of water used to baptize should not divide us, nor believing that the passage about being buried in baptism in Romans 6 should be seen as the controlling New Testament image, it is true that Anglicans have been mean about the amount of water that we have customarily used for a ceremony that speaks richly of the Red Sea, the deep waters of death, the new birth and the washing away of the past.

Over the last few years we have begun, in response to popular request, to use more water. First we offered pouring as an alternative to sprinkling for adult candidates. We covered a child's paddling pool with a white sheet, asked the candidate to stand in it and poured a quantity of water from the great baptismal brass ewer, thus thoroughly soaking him or her. As the frescoes of the earliest house churches depict baptism by pouring, this was a satisfying thing to do. I remember at one confirmation and adult baptism when, faced with a very tall candidate and a very short bishop, we had to produce a stool to enable the bishop to pour the water. Soon we progressed to a wooden tank, built by a gifted carpenter in the congregation. The symbolism was dramatic; I will never forget the first time when a family went through the waters together.

WEDDINGS

I have never met an engaged couple who have not taken their wedding plans seriously. Perhaps even approaching a vicar weeds out the casual. We offer a course for young couples, led by a doctor and her husband, which deals with both the practical business of setting up home together and acts as an introduction to the Love that they seek to keep them together for the rest of their lives. It is a good course and couples who take it learn much from their hosts and from each other. But, such is the pressure on young working people, it is rare that both have the free evenings, and rarer still for one to opt to go to the course on his or her own. The churches of England, alas, have no organized referral system; so very often a couple is married in one part of the country and then moves to another where nobody knows that they have just had a Christian wedding.

All the busy vicar can do for most couples is to make the preparation, the rehearsal and the wedding itself so meaningful that later on, they will remember and approach a local church with their children. I have been blessed with a verger and other colleagues who do their utmost to make the ceremony itself a doorway into heaven. A neighbouring vicar was encouraged when he paid a baptism visit on a couple who had been married in his church. They showed him a clip from their wedding video and the wife said, 'Every time we have cross words I get this out and we have a little cry together!' Because of the increasing breakdown in family life, there is always a poignancy about church weddings. People seem to listen intently to the address; it is a great opportunity to talk about our need for faithfulness in all relationships, and God as the source of all true faithfulness.

FUNERALS

The little white coffin was carried into church by the undertaker. On one side were the young parents with their children and their families from all over the country, some of them weeping uncontrollably; on the other were church members come to support. The funeral of a baby, just a fortnight after the baptism, is a hard thing. But few people realize how important funerals are. Often curates and others arrive in our parish in mid-life and are staggered by their first experience of the funeral of a church member. Such powerful emotions are released; such deep feelings are verbalized and ritualized. Somehow to be there, to hear the promises of Scripture about the defeat of the Last Enemy, and to sing hymns and songs of praise in the face of the apparent victory of pain and suffering, make one feel as if it is the most important thing in the world.

The Reader welcomed the family and spent a few moments explaining the context: the last time that the family was all together was for the celebration of God's love and faithfulness in baptism; now there is a more poignant celebration. Then she addressed the children: 'Your little sister has gone, but she will be always with you; her little body in the coffin is like a stretchy suit that she has outgrown and needs no more.' There was hardly a dry eye as we sang one of the songs of praise we had sung at the baptism.

Most Anglican funerals are of those people who have little or no contact with the church, so that each – however routine to the undertakers and the parson – represents an opportunity for the good news, because of the tremendous significance of the death of that individual to the friends and family. Jesus said, 'Let the dead bury the dead', and the gospel, which is about life in all its fullness, can be compromised if too much time and energy are spent on funerals to the neglect of the church; but handling death with realism, compassion and hope is something that the church is uniquely qualified to do. In my present parish we do not normally have more than two dozen funerals a year, and so we can afford to take time and trouble with the funerals that come our way.

People listen hard at funerals. There are big questions and worries on many hearts. The challenge is to speak into their hearts without compromising the gospel or manipulating people at vulnerable moments in their lives. There are delicate judgements to be made about whether this poem or reading is suitable (not Scott Holland, please!) this music allowable (not 'I did it my way!') or whether that person can make a proper tribute (will he be sober?). The minister has to be able to cope with anguish when the curtains close at the crematorium, or with disputes about the will over the open grave. But people will not forget a few well-chosen words about the hope of resurrection. Part of the privilege of the local pastoral ministry is that over the years a very substantial part of the population of the parish will come through the doors of the church. If there is the right mix of hospitality and proclamation many of them will look towards their local church for help when trouble comes.

COUNSELLING

One of the fruits of the Spirit is the giving of wise counsel.[23] When people are touched by God they will approach their church leaders for advice about reordering their lives. A sure way to prevent growth in a community is for the ordained ministers to be the only ones who give this counsel. An even better way is for the minister to take a degree in counselling and to spend his or her afternoons in seeing clients. Professional counselling is quite distinct from the spiritual counsel that a housegroup leader or spiritual guide can give, and confusing the two can severely damage the health of a church.

Professional counselling has developed greatly recently and is an important resource for the local church. Housegroup leaders and the prayer ministry team will need to know when to refer people on to this specialist help. The church will want to have a list of qualified counsellors who can be approached over particular problems, plus sums of money to help pay for them. Therapies are not value-neutral and the church will check that the professionals are operating within a worldview that is not antithetical to the biblical understanding of our fallen nature and our need of redemption.[24] Equally a local church will want to be on its guard against some of the excesses of a therapeutic culture that believes that whatever helps you must be right and whatever hurts you must be wrong.[25] For a useful guide to what is available and for advice about how to use counselling to promote true healing and renewal, see *Counselling in Context* by Francis Bridger and David Atkinson.[26]

BEING FAMILY

The calling of the Christian Church is to be an alternative human family, a community of love, fulfilling the promise made to Abraham long ago. In theory we churches take damaged human beings in whom the image of God has been marred, introduce them to the Lord, see them come to faith and wholeness and then in their turn reach out to their neighbours. The two great commandments – to love God with all our hearts and to love our neighbours as ourselves – are at the heart of everything we stand for. And yet in practice we find that pride and selfishness survive in our churches, along with the other seven deadly sins. If churches are not growing, the problem is not usually lack of evangelism but lack of love. We do not always hear people saying, 'How those Christians love one another', but rather 'I don't go to church because of all the unpleasantness.' In the older, more formal style of churchgoing, when you met for an hour or so on Sunday and often knew people only from the back of their heads, this could be overlooked but, now that a deeper kind of community life is yearned for, the shortcomings of Christians are exposed. The disintegration of traditional community life in the West provides a tremendous opportunity for the churches, and failure at this point renders empty every other kind of attempt at being an outward-looking and hospitable community.

Florence Allshorn, pioneer missionary and founder of the St Julian's Community in Sussex, has written as movingly as anyone in the last hundred years about this problem, finding that she could not be an effective missionary because she could not live and work well with her fellow missionaries. She wrote from the African bush school but she could have been describing the leadership team of an English church. Florence was brought to despair. It was clear that she might as well go back to England for all the good she was doing. She was not bringing the Spirit of Jesus to the school. The children were fully aware that the atmosphere was wrong. She had come to the crisis of her life.

I was young and I was the eighth youngster who had been sent, none of whom had lasted more than two years. I went down to seven stone and my spirit and soul wilted to the same degree. Then one day the old African matron came to me when I was sitting on the veranda crying my eyes out. She said, 'I have been on this station for fifteen years and I have seen you come out, all of you saying you have brought to us a Saviour, but I have never seen this situation saved yet.' It brought me to my senses with a bang. I was the problem for myself. I knew enough of Jesus Christ to know that the enemy was the one to be loved before you could call yourself a follower of Jesus Christ, and I prayed, in great ignorance as to what it might do, that this same love might be in me, and I prayed as I have never prayed in my life for that one thing.[27]

She decided to stay after all. Something changed in her in a way that was so profound that she found it difficult to talk about but became the basis of all her future ministry in building community, in teaching about it at Selly Oak Missionary Training College, and in enabling thousands of exhausted pastors and missionaries to find fresh inspiration at St Julian's, Coolham. Her biographer recounts that she simply decided to love and to let Christ save the situation through her. For a whole year she read 1 Corinthians 13 every day. 'Life became an adventure in learning to love instead of the agony it had been before.' The older missionary became a friend instead of an enemy, and the hated school became a home, the first real home that Florence had experienced since leaving her own family.

Local churches and their leaders need religious communities for several reasons, but one is that they are practised at dealing with the human ego at close quarters and have built up a fund of knowledge and experience. Many of the charismatic church communities of the 1970s foundered not because the ideal was wrong but simply because they were ignorant of church history and tried to do too much too soon. When Florence Allshorn started St Julian's with three colleagues it was with the same adventure of learning to love in mind.

> What carried us through was that we had said that we would not leave if we found ourselves in a bad patch, and that we would not accept defeat . . . When people talk about starting communities we look at each other. They seem to us like people starting for the North Pole without even knowing that they need a warm coat.[28]

What all communities discover if they persevere is that love is not the absence of conflict, but something that is found on the other side of conflict, if conflict is honestly faced. So many church communities fail because there is no mechanism for persevering, and the relationships are all voluntary; we duck out and disappear rather than go on to find the crock of gold. It is only when people are willing to be bound together for the sake of the gospel that they can reach beyond the superficiality to the reality.

In Henry Nouwen's meditation on Rembrandt's great painting, *Return of the Prodigal Son*,[29] he shows how a truly Christian pastoral care will identify with each of the three main characters in the painting. We will continue to identify with the prodigal younger son: any pastoral care that has forgotten its own need of repentance and healing becomes pharisaic or bureaucratic. We will continue to identify with the elder brother: to acknowledge our own inner stiffness and our intolerance of newcomers. But we will also start to identify with the loving and forgiving Father whose whole being is given over to welcome and forgiveness; we will grow up into maturity where we will not just be part of the Church as woolly lambs seeking comfort, but will also be willing to be God's servants, offering friendship and love to the unlovely.

YOUTH AND CHILDREN

There has been a fall in Sunday-school attendance from 50 per cent of the population in the 1940s to under 5 per cent today. Has it been altogether a coincidence that youth crime has risen as dramatically as Sunday-school attendance has fallen during the same period? Looking back over two decades of parish work I am clear that the provision of high-quality children's and youth work has been one of the most important features of growing a church family and serving the wider parish. Forty years ago children could walk on their own to church, so their clubs could be held at times independent of the Sunday services. These days parents will not let their children roam freely so Sunday school has to be at the same time as church services. Sometimes it is healthy for all ages to worship together. But children also need to worship and be taught at their own pace. One of the assumptions behind some recent church reports has been that a few well-behaved children can, with the help of soft toys, sit quietly through Parish Communion. But if, as has happened to us, seven-year-olds invite all their friends, they will need their own time.

In each church where we have served, we have reorganized the Sunday school (under many different names, of course) so that the worship begins and ends with all ages together, but that the various age groups separate for the ministry of the word. Much has depended on parents and others being willing to take responsibility for organizing the children's work. Children's work has to be budgeted for. The materials are not expensive if the labour is free, but the costs mount up. At one of our churches we had no money for leaflets until a generous donation arrived unexpectedly from the manager of the local cinema to thank us for bringing large audiences to a Christian film. After this pump-priming we were able to pay for the leaflets. The pattern of growth has been similar in each place we have worked. First the church has prayed for the right team of volunteers and spent time and energy on their support. I knew we had it right when a young woman approached me after a service to tell me how incompetent I was at organizing the children! She then masterminded one of the best children's Sunday schools ever. The result was that children came more regularly. Where parents used to come perhaps once a month each, they then changed over time to both coming each week. Then the children have invited their friends. The leaders and helpers have found their own faith and knowledge greatly deepened through having to teach; often they have also come to the evening service to join in the adult worship they have missed in the morning. Once numbers have started to rise and the children enjoy themselves, it is easy for enquirers and newcomers to bring their own children.

Recent legislation to protect children from abuse has added to the difficulties of running large-scale children's work. But, difficult though it is, children's and youth work is so important that almost any sacrifice of time and effort is worth while. The Church should offer womb-to-tomb care – lifelong learning indeed. The effects can be startling. I remember driving with a hard-nosed policeman round his beat; he made a point of telling me about one area where youth crime had dropped significantly after the church there had started an open youth club. We hold a children's holiday Bible club at the end of the long summer vacation. It is a great amount of work for all those involved, but we keep going if only because the teachers at the local primary school told us when we started that it made such a positive difference to the children's behaviour. A new development in recent years has been after-school clubs. Because weekends are more crowded and fewer parents are at home when schools end, churches that provide high-quality children's clubs in the early evening have found a ready market, and parents are deeply grateful to them.

Youth work grows naturally out of children's work. Where do our children go for recreation and for growth in discipleship when they have outgrown the junior church? Youth work is even more tribal than children's work because teenagers are starting to be independent of parents; it is with this age group that the question of what touches people-groups rather than individuals is at its most pressing. It is important to encourage the young people to worship God in their own idiom. I treasure the moment when a junior youth leader told me that because the older people had allowed his contemporaries to take over the church for youth services, the youth had started to appreciate the music that the older people liked.

Although every church, however small, needs its own crèche and Sunday school, it is more difficult for rural churches and small urban ones to organize their own youth work unless they combine with their neighbours. Because clergy are generally older than they used to be it is important to find leaders for youth work younger than most curates. Many churches have solved this problem by combining together to fund youth ministers. Some of the best we have had have been people who have just graduated and are willing to give a year or two to the young people of a church in return for accommodation and pocket money. Other churches hire youth workers who have a qualification in youth or community work. This is more expensive but often results after very few years in a youth work that grows to over 50 and makes a real impact on the neighbourhood.

The next question, unfaced as yet by most churches, is how to enable those young people to hear God about their own calling, to take up leadership roles in the Church at home and abroad, to join the governance of their church, and to learn how to make relationships which will last. Here the large national events like Greenbelt, Spring Harvest and Soul Survivor are helpfully modelling what being a young disciple of Christ can mean. If the tradition is right that suggests that the Virgin Mary and the apostle John were both in their mid-teens when they were called upon by God to make life-changing decisions, perhaps we could be more adventurous in the challenges we offer to our young people.

HEALING

If children's work has been one of the key growth points for my congregations, sickness and healing have been another. We have lived publicly for several generations in a closed universe where a demonstrable and verifiable cause exists for every effect and where there is therefore no room for supernatural intervention. Years ago people prayed for rain; now they wait for the weather forecast to announce a depression. Once there were witches and spells; now there are mental hospitals and psychiatrists. Or so runs the argument. In public the idea that God heals in answer to prayer is an embarrassment. In private, however, the intelligent newspapers have quietly introduced horoscopes to their pages; and all the surveys show that scientific materialism does not appeal to many – if it ever did.

Recently a woman came into the vestry to see me. She has been a stalwart in our church for over 30 years, runs a women's group and cooks for a lunch club of 40 elderly people every week. She is a practical person and not always immediately happy about some of the changes that the charismatic movement has brought to her church. A year ago, she reminded me, she was at a meeting when the subject of miracles was mentioned; she had said publicly, 'I have been a member of this church for 32 years and I have never seen a miracle.' Then she found herself asking for prayer for the migraine attack that was starting. Her housegroup leader led everyone in prayer, and a year later she said, 'Do you know, it went instantly. I have had migraines for 20 years, but through all this last year I have not had one.'

Those who are trapped in a closed universe are deprived of wonderful answers to prayer and beautiful healings. Of course by definition a miracle is something that happens exceptionally. Physical healings through prayer alone are the exception rather than the rule. In this life we have a foretaste of heaven, enough of the supernatural to encourage our faith in a God who is Lord over death and bringer of wholeness, but we all weaken and die, and we need as much medical help as we can get. We walk by faith, not by the bribery of cures on demand. If people's faith is severely shaken because prayers for physical healing are not answered then their faith is wrongly based. Our faith begins with a death, matures with a dying to self, and includes a coming to terms with our own mortality. Our family and friends are not a permanent possession; they are lent to us for a day at a time, and what counts is not the length of the loan but the quality of the relationship. We pray for healing because of the command of the Lord to his apostles, not because we can guarantee results.

But in practice prayer for healing almost always brings tangible results – an easing of pain here, a taking away of worry there, a shortening of the time of convalescence or a beautiful and visionary dying. These may seem like a let-out to the agnostic or a delusion and hypocrisy to the atheist, but to sufferers and their friends they are no small mercy. And in addition there is in any reasonably sized church much more than that; a trickle of quite surprising and wonderful answers to prayer that touch the hearts of all but the most sceptical.

In my first curacy a woman of about 30 came to see my vicar and me; she had inoperable cancer of the womb and had been given six weeks to live. She came and wept over us and cried out that she did not want to die and leave her husband and children. Although not a churchgoer she was a midwife and had delivered the children of many families in the parish. The churchwarden's wife was a great person of prayer and her youngest child had been delivered by this woman; so she set about praying and fasting. We gathered people to pray and arranged to go and anoint and lay hands on the woman. Afterwards I remember driving back and thinking to myself, 'She is going to die.' But my vicar and the churchwarden's wife had more faith, and we all kept on praying. When she went back to the Christie Hospital for her next check-up the consultant thought he had been given the wrong X-ray, so dramatic was the improvement. 'It is a great puzzle,' he said, not finding the vocabulary of signs and wonders to hand, 'an unaccountable remission.' First she and then her husband were soundly converted, and the 'remission' has lasted over 25 years.

Faith is not a commodity to be found on the shelf of the church bookstall. It is more like a muscle that needs to be exercised; perhaps a muscle that needs physiotherapy because it has become atrophied in the Church today. God reaches down as we reach up to him and surprises us. I have no particular gifts in this area but have seen enough encouraging miracles to know that the gift of healing did not cease when the first generation of apostles died.

DELIVERANCE

The message on the answerphone from the hospital chaplain sounded urgent. A hospital employee had had a series of accidents that she had begun to attribute to a curse; when the chaplain had called she too was convinced that something was wrong in the house; would I visit and help with a service of Holy Communion? I consulted the person appointed by the bishop to oversee questions of deliverance. Then I invited the chaplain to join us for Evening Prayer when the staff team prayed for guidance as to how to proceed. The next day she, one of our Readers and I met at the house and heard again from the woman, and from her sister and brother-in-law. They too suggested sources of the sudden cold and frightening atmosphere in the house, which both sisters felt and which the chaplain had also noticed. One was a kind of curse from a woman who had a relationship with an ex-partner of the householder; the other was Uncle W who had died in the house ten years before and whose benign but continuing presence had been credited with occasional disturbances of furniture. The sisters had strong religious beliefs but had not been churchgoers as adults and did not speak of a living relationship with Christ. The husband said he would go along with anything that helped his wife and sister-in-law.

The chaplain handled the situation sensitively but definitely. She suggested a three-pronged plan of action. First, there would be a simple service of Holy Communion at the heart of which would be the proclamation of Christ's victory on the cross over the powers of evil. Second, we would formally lay Uncle W to rest in case for any reason he was not in the place he was meant to be. And third, we would pray for the house and its cleansing by going from room to room and sprinkling holy water as a sign of God's power to drive out any uncleanness. They agreed with some enthusiasm. Afterwards I did not feel anything at all, but those we had come to help were sure that business had been done and that they could now grieve properly for their uncle. The chaplain ended by suggesting a rose might be planted in his memory and as there is a rose with his name that seemed appropriate. Two weeks later the chaplain, the Reader and I had a debriefing session to go over what had happened. She had had a meal with the woman who was delighted with the new-found peace in her home. I heard this from her myself when she came to see me to ask if she might be confirmed.

Request for prayer for hauntings, spiritual disturbance, exorcisms and the like have been much rarer than requests for prayer for healing, which is a regular part of local church ministry. But the spiritual battle is real enough and it is as well to be prepared and to have some training and good practice available for when cases do arise. Over the years we have seen a small number of people delivered from otherwise unaccountable symptoms who have in their past been involved unwittingly in occult practices. We have prayed for them authoritatively and they have been released. In this field above all others it is important to be under authority.[30]

CONCLUSION

There are so many aspects to building Christian community and so many different gifts and skills which have to be used that it is hard to know where to stop writing about them. However, the discerning reader will have noticed two particular omissions in these chapters. The first is any proper mention of the 'post-modernity' debate. While the features that make up the concept of post-modernity (the loss of the grand narrative, the fragmentation of personality, the pick-and-mix philosophies, the breakdown in community) are part of the contemporary landscape and appear frequently in these pages, the thesis that we live in a post-modern age remains unconvincing and in part self-contradictory. Has not the theory of post-modernity become itself a kind of *grand récit*, particularly in Christian circles? Most of the so-called features of post-modernity are there in modernism; many come much earlier. Who could be more of a post-modern than Hamlet? Is it not true that the New Testament narratives themselves exhibit some of the key features of post-modernity? Consumerism and globalization act together as a seductive philosophy of the western mindset and Christian thinkers should not be too easily seduced.

The second omission in these pages is any systematic treatment of 'new ways of being Church'. Missionaries as different as Vincent Donovan and Roland Allen have urged that, just as St Paul allowed the new communities of believers to develop their own customs and ways of worship, so we should build churches which encourage Christians to 'be Church' in quite different ways from the 'inherited mode'.[31] This New Testament missionary principle is being fruitfully applied not only to different people groups but also to youth work, treating young people as a kind of separate tribe. There are many useful books on this topic and an excellent series of articles by George Lings available from Church Army entitled *Encounters on the Edge* gives specific examples from different parts of the UK. The reason for not adding to the literature here is not because the arguments are unconvincing. Every church should be taking risks and pioneering in some way or other, for the sake of all those people who will never find God through traditional church services. However, the more I see of the experiments the more I believe that, alongside necessary and inspiring experimentation, more ordinary and even traditional congregational life can and does flourish, given the right conditions. There is no necessary conflict between the so-called 'emerging generation' Church and the 'traditional' Church. In most places it should be 'both/and' rather than 'either/or'. There is particularly no need for church leaders to feel second-rate if their congregations are at the centre of their community and the community is responding to the Good News in the traditional way.

All ministry is like the seed falling to the ground in the parable that Jesus told when some Greeks came to enquire about him: 'Very truly, I tell you, unless a grain of wheat falls into the earth and dies, it remains just a single grain; but if it dies, it bears much fruit.'[32] Modern urban people have forgotten the reality behind this image. In an agricultural society one is faced with a painful choice when it comes to the last of the grain in the family granary each year. Either the family can go hungry and put that grain in to the ground for next year's bread, or it can use the grain for bread now and starve next year. Jesus is saying that in our ministries all of us have a similar choice: *either* to fulfil our own desires but then to find our church dying, *or* to follow the Lord on his way of the cross, to die to some of our own plans and desires, so that 'much fruit' results. For any Christian community to grow, for there to be new people coming to faith, a church needs a whole host of people who will offer love to the youth, to the sick, to the newcomers, so that they experience the local church as a place where the generosity of God is met.

Once there was a young widow in our church who was lonely; as she prayed to God about her life, he said to her, 'If you need love, show love.' As he spoke to her she saw in her mind many other people in need of new relationships; she became a wonderful host and people blossomed and became friends in her home. She was a grain that bore much fruit.

In the same passage Jesus says, 'When I am lifted up, I will draw all people to me.' Real love attracts like nothing else. That is the heart of pastoral care. Real love also turns enquirers into disciples. Unlooked-for care challenges us to commitment.

Jesus goes on to say, 'Whoever serves me must follow me, and where I am, there will my servant be also. Whoever serves me, the Father will honour.' Jesus' divine love is transferable. His sacrificial love trains us for ministry. When the cross is set up in our hearts, Christ's love can be transferred from person to person and generation to generation.

The great paradox of life, both for individuals and for communities, is that when we flit about searching for ourselves and preserving our own status we lose ourselves and 'die alone'. When individuals and churches are willing to die to that superficial self, we find our real selves in God.

The good seed of the gospel always bears fruit. God's word never returns to him empty without accomplishing his purpose. People in our time and culture are desperate for something more than the consumer culture. In fact the whole creation still waits with eager longing for the revealing of the children of God in real Christian community life. As a result there will be much fruit in that community which Christ's love builds in the Age of the Spirit. Leading a local church is like encouraging the crew to hoist the sails on a boat. Maybe nothing happens at first. But, if the sail is well trimmed, sooner or later we will be sailing: going places together.

Notes

I BEING A LEADER

1 'Prayers after the Birth of a still-born Child', *Alternative Service Book* (London, SPCK; Clowes, Cambridge University Press, 1980), p. 322; cf. *Common Worship Pastoral Services* (London, The Archbishops' Council, Church House Publishing), p. 302.

2 The church at Willow Creek, Chicago, developed intelligent 'Seekers' Services' designed to answer the questions of enquirers and new-comers. See Martin Robinson, *A World Apart: Creating a Church for the Unchurched: Learning from Willow Creek* (Crowborough, Monarch, 1992).

3 John 10.11; 21.17–19 (RSV).

4 Luke 12.32.

5 Psalm 23.

6 See, for instance, Luke 12.32; 15.3–7.

7 cf. 'Thou on earth both priest and victim in the eucharistic feast' from S. S. Wesley's hymn, 'Alleluia! sing to Jesus!'

8 Revelation 5.6.

9 John 1.36; 10.11.

10 Revelation 5.12.

11 Romans 1.10; Ephesians 1.7–10.

12 Acts 2.17.

13 Romans 15.18.

14 'Whoever would be first among you must be slave of all' (Mark 10.44, RSV).

15 Raymond E. Brown, *The Churches the Apostles Left Behind* (Ramsey, NY, Paulist Press, 1984).

16 Philippians 2.5–7.

17 John 13.14.

18 See, for instance, Christopher Hill, *The English Bible and the Seven-teenth-Century Revolution* (London, Penguin, 1993).

19 Galatians 2.11–18.

20 Acts 10.

21 Matthew 10.33.

22 John 21.18.

23 Matthew 16.23 (RSV).

24 This might be suggested by Graham Kendrick's song, 'I will build my church', where the first part of the verse, 'You are Peter, and on this rock . . .' is mysteriously airbrushed out!

25 Romans 8.36 (NRSV).

26 See, especially, Robert K. Greenleaf, *The Power of Servant Leadership* (San Francisco, Berrett-Koehler, 1998). Compare with Stephen Croft, *Ministry in Three Dimensions: Ordination and Leadership in the Local Church* (London, Darton, Longman & Todd, 1999).

27 2 Corinthians 3.18; Philippians 1.6.

28 Vincent J. Donovan, *Christianity Rediscovered: An Epistle from the Masai* (London, SCM Press, 1978).

29 H. P. Liddon, *Clerical Life and Work* (London, Longmans, Green & Co., 1903), p. 46.

30 Isaiah 50.4.

31 Liddon, *Clerical Life*, p. 49 (shortened).

32 Gordon MacDonald, *Ordering Your Private World* (Crowborough, Highland Books, 1985), p. 81.

33 Edmund Morgan, Bishop of Southampton, 1943–51.

34 Mark 13.32.

35 Michael Polanyi, *Personal Knowledge: Towards a Post-Critical Philosophy* (London, Routledge & Kegan Paul, 1958).

36 Acts 19.8–9.

37 Joyce Huggett, *Listening to God* (London, Hodder, 1986).

38 1 Thessalonians 5.19–21.

2 THE AGE OF THE SPIRIT

1 'Rite A', *Alternative Service Book* (London, SPCK; Clowes, Cambridge University Press, 1980); and 'Order 1', *Common Worship Pastoral Services* (London, The Archbishops' Council, Church House Publishing, 2000).

2 Exodus 33.16 (RSV).

3 Lesslie Newbigin, *The Household of God* (London, SCM Press, 1953), p. 87.

4 Newbigin, *Household*, p. 89.

5 1 John 3.24 (NRSV).

6 John 7.37–39 (NRSV).

7 Jeremiah 2.13 (NRSV). See also Exodus 17; Psalm 63.1; Isaiah 55 among many other passages.

8 Ezekiel 47.1–12; cf. Revelation 22.1–2.

9   See Tom Wright, *Jesus and the Victory of God* (London, SPCK, 1996).

10 See, for instance, *The Charismatic Movement in the Church of England* (London, CIO Publishing, 1981), p. 9.

11 Acts 2.17.

12 John Robinson, *Honest to God* (London, SCM Press, 1963).

13 David Wilkerson, *The Cross and the Switchblade* (New York, Spire; London, Marshall Pickering, London, 1963).

14 P. T. O'Brien, *Ephesians* (Leicester, IVP, 1999).

15 Ephesians 4.16.

16 Ephesians 4.7–16.

17 Interestingly this list is quoted twice in the service of the Ordination of Priests in the Book of Common Prayer.

18 Ephesians 4.12.

19 See *Good News People*, a report of the House of Bishops (London, Church House Publishing, 1999).

20 Ephesians 4.12–13.

21 Ephesians 4.16.

22 See, for instance, John Snow, *The Impossible Vocation: Ministry in the Mean Time* (Cambridge, MA, Cowley Publications, 1988), p. 38.

23 See, for instance, Ken and Lois Gott, *The Sunderland Revival* (London, Hodder & Stoughton, 1995); and also George Lings, *Encounters on the Edge*, especially No. 1 in the series: 'Living Proof' (Sheffield, Church Army, 1999).

24 Revelation 3.20.

25 See Guy Chevreau, *The Toronto Blessing* (London, Marshall Pickering, 1994), for a sympathetic account, and Martyn Percy, *Words, Wonders and Power* (London, SPCK, 1996), for a critical assessment.

26 P. Dixon, 'Medical Perspectives on Manifestations', in P. Dixon (ed.), *Signs of Revival* (Eastbourne, Kingsway, 1994), p. 133.

27 Acts 10.

28 See John Drury, *Painting the Word* (New Haven and London, Yale University Press, 1999), for reproductions of these two works, though Drury would not make a point as unsubtle as this.

29 See, for instance, Hudson Taylor, *Union and Communion* (London, Religious Tract Society, 1929).

30 1 Thessalonians 4.20–2, my translation.

3 LEADING UNCOMMON WORSHIP

1   Psalm 145.10 (NRSV).

2   Evelyn Underhill, *Worship* (London, Nisbet & Co., 1936).

3 T. S. Eliot, 'The Hollow Men', 1925, in *Collected Poems 1909–1962* (London, Faber, 1963).

4 Psalm 19.1.

5 1 Peter 2.10.

6 C. S. Lewis, *Reflections on the Psalms* (London, Collins/Fontana, 1961), p. 80.

7 Luke 19.40.

8 Hebrews 2.8–9.

9 Romans 8.19, 26.

10 Romans 8.23 (NRSV).

11 Phil Rogers, *How to be a Worshipper* (Hove, Coastlands, 1984), p. 33. The 'new' churches are what we used to call 'house' churches until they grew too big to meet in homes. They are an important and lively part of the ecumenical scene today and in some areas are the only effective Christian churches.

12 Exodus 12.26–7 (NRSV).

13 Acts 2.42.

14 Acts 4.25–6.

15 Revelation 5.9 ff.

16 2 Corinthians 3.17 (REB).

17 Ian Robinson, *The Survival of English* (Cambridge, Cambridge University Press, 1973), p. 38.

18 Robin Sheldon (ed.), *In Spirit and in Truth* (London, Hodder, 1989), p. 47.

19 *Faith in the City* (London, Church House Publishing, 1985), p. 66.

20 See, for instance, William Edgar, *Taking Note of Music* (London, SPCK, 1986), p. 131, or Graham Cray, 'Justice, Rock and the Renewal of Worship' in Sheldon, *In Spirit*, p. 16.

21 John 4.23 (RSV).

22 2 Samuel 6.14–21.

23 1 Corinthians 14.26.

24 Wesley Carr, *The Priestlike Task* (London, SPCK, 1985).

25 1 Corinthians 14.26 (RSV).

26 Matthew 13.52 (RSV).

4 PREACHING – HANDING ON THE VISION

1 Christian Schwarz, *Natural Church Development* (Beds., British Church Growth Association, 1996).

2 Prompted by a conversation with M. P. M. Booker, author of *Exploring Natural Church Development* (Cambridge, Grove, 2001).

3 For example, D. Nineham, *The Use and Abuse of the Bible* (London, SPCK, 1986).

4 Claus Westermann, *The Old Testament and Jesus Christ* (Minneapolis, MN, Augsburg, 1968).

5 John Wimber, *Power Evangelism* (London, Hodder, 1985).

6 Oral Roberts, *The Call: An Autobiography* (London, Hodder, 1972).

7 See, for example, Lesslie Newbigin, *A South India Diary* (London, SCM Press, 1951).

8 Acts 2.16 (AV).

9 Matthew 11.29–30.

10 *Documents of Vatican II*, pp. 538–9, cited in the Pontifical Bible Commission, *The Interpretation of the Bible in the Church* (Montreal, QC, Editions Paulines, 1994).

11 H. W. Robinson, *Expository Preaching* (Leicester, IVP, 1986).

12 Robinson, *Expository Preaching*, p. 67.

13 *The Bible Speaks Again*, trans. Annebeth Mackie (London, SCM Press, 1969), p. 122.

14 Koyama, *Waterbuffalo Theology*, quoted in S. B. Bevans, *Models of Contextual Theology* (New York, Orbis Books, 1992).

15 See the helpful Bill Hybels, *Mastering Contemporary Preaching* (Leicester, IVP, 1991).

16 Ezekiel 2.8—3.4.

17 Acts 4.13.

18 Floyd McClung, *The Father Heart of God* (Eastbourne, Kingsway, 1985).

19 As suggested in G. Theissen, *The Shadow of the Galilean* (London, SCM Press, 1987), p. 124.

20 This chapter was drafted before I discovered David Day's *A Preaching Workbook* (London, SPCK, 1999). It is the book I wish I could have written and says far more convincingly than I have what needs to be said about the craft of preaching.

5 MAKING DISCIPLES

1 William Beckham, *The Second Reformation* (Houston, TX, Touch Publications, 1995); Ian Freestone, *A New Way of Being Church* (Balgowlah, Australia, Sold Out Publications, 1995); Howard Astin, *Body and Cell* (Crowborough, Monarch, 1998). The values behind the cell church are gospel values, which work well in pioneering situations where there is no established church; churches that seek to 'transition' from housegroups to cells are not as yet finding it easy – but the experiment is worthwhile, because many housegroups have settled back into being discussion groups.

2 See Peter Ball, *The Adult Way to Faith* (London, Mowbray, 1992); *On the Way: Towards an Integrated Approach to Christian Initiation* (Report for General Synod GS Misc 444 – London, Church House Publishing, 1995); John Finney, *Finding Faith Today* (Swindon, Bible Society, 1992).

3 Michael Wooderson, *The Church Down Our Street* (Eastbourne, Marc Europe [Monarch], 1989).

4 See Alice Fryling, *Disciple-Makers' Handbook* (Leicester, IVP, 1989).

5 Lesley Edmonds, *Volunteers: A Resource for Your Church* (Berkhamsted, The Volunteer Centre UK, 1988).

6 David Watson, later to become Vicar of St Michael-le-Belfry, York, and an outstanding evangelist.

7 David Sheppard, later to become Bishop of Liverpool.

8 John Harvey-Jones, *Does Industry Matter?* (London, BBC Books, 1986), p. 11.

9 Lindsay Mackay, obituary in *Weekly Guardian*, 2 October 1994.

6 SERVING THE WORLD ON YOUR DOORSTEP

1 John Ruskin, *Unto This Last* (Harmondsworth, Penguin, 1985); William Booth, *In Darkest England and the Way Out* (London, The Salvation Army, 1890).

2 See, for example, Deuteronomy 10.16–22; 15.1–6.

3 Luke 16.19–31.

4 See the helpful discussion in Paul Avis, *Church, State and Establishment* (London, SPCK, 2001).

5 *Faith in the City* (London, Church House Publishing, 1985); cf. *God in the City: Essays and Reflections from the Archbishop of Canterbury's Urban Theology Group* (London, Mowbray, 1985); Anthony Harvey (ed.), *Theology in the City* (London, SPCK, 1989); *Staying in the City: Faith in the City Ten Years On*, a report by the Bishops' Advisory Group on Urban Priority Areas (London, Church House Publishing, 1995); Eric Blakebrough (ed.), *Church for the City* (London, Darton, Longman & Todd, 1995); *Faith in the Countryside: Report of the Archbishops' Commission on Rural Areas (ACORA)* (Worthing, Churchman Publishing, 1990).

6 The word 'dwell' or 'camp' in the Johannine writings is not unconnected with the idea of the 'sojourner'; in our terms, 'migrant' or 'asylum seeker'.

7 Pecan Ltd, 1 Atwell Rd, London SE15 4TW, www.pecan.org.uk

8 *Knocking at Heaven's Door, The CARIS report on the Casual Caller* (London, London Diocesan Board for Social Responsibility, 1996).

9 See, for instance, David Sheppard, *Built as a City* (London, Hodder

& Stoughton, 1974); Michael Eastman, *Ten Inner-City Churches* (Eastbourne, Kingsway, 1988).

10 See, for instance, Raymond Fung, *The Isaiah Vision* (Geneva, WCC Publications, 1992).

11 Ann Morisy, *Beyond the Good Samaritan* (London, Mowbray, 1997).

12 See, for instance, Geiko Müller-Fahrenholz, *The Art of Forgiveness: Theological Reflections on Healing and Reconciliation* (Geneva, WCC Publications, 1997).

13 *Faith in the City*, p. 360.

7 MISSION AND EVANGELISM

1 Walter Brueggemann, *Biblical Perspectives on Evangelism* (Nashville, TN, Abingdon Press, 1993).

2 Most magisterial and convincing has been David Bosch, *Transforming Mission* (New York, Orbis, 1991).

3 John 15.16; Matthew 28.19–20.

4 See Paul Avis, *Church, State and Establishment* (London, SPCK, 2001).

5 See, for instance, Walter Brueggemann, *The Prophetic Imagination* (Philadelphia, PA, Fortress Press, 1978).

6 Eloquently written about by Lesslie Newbigin, *The Gospel in a Pluralist Society* (London, SPCK, 1989).

7 Ben Hatch, *The Lawnmower Celebrity* (London, Victor Gollancz, 2000).

8 2 Corinthians 2.14.

9 Words now introduced into the Church of England *Common Worship* Eucharist.

10 See, for instance, Eddie Gibbs, *I Believe in Church Growth* (London, Hodder, 1981).

11 See, for instance, Robert Warren, *Being Human, Being Church* (London, HarperCollins, 1995).

12 *Good News People*, a report of the House of Bishops (London, Church House Publishing, 1999). See also David Sanderson, *The Work and Office of an Evangelist* (Nottingham, Grove Books, 1995).

13 Simon Beasley, *How Friendly to Strangers is Your Church?*, privately printed in Southampton by the author, available from CPAS, Athena Drive, Tachbrook Park, Warwick CV36 6NG.

14 John Clarke, *Evangelism that Really Works* (London, SPCK, 1995), p. 100.

15 See Bruce Reed, *The Dynamics of Religion* (London, Darton, Longman & Todd, 1979).

16 See, among many others, *Breaking New Ground: Church Planting in*

the Church of England (London, Church House Publishing, 1994); Diana Archer, *Who'd Plant a Church?* (Crowborough, Christina Press, 1998); R. Allon-Smith and T. Bradley, *An MOT for Church Plants* (Cambridge, Grove Books, 1998).

17 Hebrews 12.15 (RSV).
18 Galatians 5.23.

8 MANAGING PEOPLE

1 C. S. Forester, *Hornblower and the Hotspur* (Harmondsworth, Penguin, 1968), p. 34.
2 Pius XII, *Mystici Corporis* (New York, America Press, 1957), p. 22. Andrew Lincoln, *Ephesians* (Dallas, Texas, Word Books, 1990), p. 263 agrees at least in part with Pius XII, but see also Colossians 2.19.
3 Robin Gill and Derek Burke, *Strategic Church Leadership* (London, SPCK, 1996), p. 5.
4 Dick Anderson, *We Felt Like Grasshoppers* (Nottingham, Crossway Books, 1994), p. 58.
5 Anderson, *Like Grasshoppers*, p. 59.
6 Anderson, *Like Grasshoppers*, p. 65.
7 Kenneth M. Macmorran and Timothy Briden, *A Handbook for Churchwardens and Parochial Church Councillors* (London, Mowbray, 1996).
8 Charles Handy, *Understanding Voluntary Organizations* (Harmondsworth, Penguin, 1988). See also Mike Hudson, *Managing without Profit: The Art of Managing Third-Sector Organizations* (Harmondsworth, Penguin, 1995).
9 'Profile', *Observer*, 9 October 1994, p. 26.
10 Nelson Mandela, *Long Walk to Freedom* (Boston, MA, Little, Brown & Co., 1994).
11 See Donald Bridge, *Spare the Rod and Spoil the Church* (Bromley, Marc Europe, 1985).

9 RAISING MONEY – FINANCE AND BUILDINGS

1 Richard Giles, *Re-Pitching the Tent* (Norwich, Canterbury Press, 1995).

10 THE CLERICAL PROFESSION

1 E. Schillebeeckx, *Ministry* (London, SCM Press, 1980), p. 15.
2 *Recovering Confidence: The Call to Ordained Ministry in a Changing World*, ABM Ministry Paper No. 13 (London, CBF, 1996).

3 A common misquote from Ignatius, *Ad. Smyrn.*VIII. What Ignatius wrote was, 'Wherever the bishop appears, there let the people be, even as wherever Christ Jesus is, there is the catholic church.'

4 Matthew 18.20 (RSV).

5 'Stipendiary Ordinations 1879–1999' (figure), in G. Kuhrt, *Ministry Issues for the Church of England* (London, Church House Publishing, 2001), p. 93.

6 Matthew 10.35—11.1.

7 John 15.12–17.

8 *Recovering Confidence*, §57.

9 'Where there is real love, there Christian ministry will emerge' (to modify the well-known Taizé song).

10 *Recovering Confidence*, §41.

11 *Youth A Part*, a report on young people and the church produced jointly by the National Society and Church House Publishing (London, 1996).

12 John Harvey-Jones, *Does Industry Matter?* (London, BBC Books, 1986), p. 11.

13 Anthony Russell, *The Clerical Profession* (London, SPCK, 1980).

14 Richard Turnbull (ed.), *Generosity and Sacrifice*, A Church of England Consultative Report to the Dioceses (2001).

15 I. T. Ramsey, *Words About God* (London, SCM Press, 1971); and Thomas Kuhn, *The Structure of Scientific Revolutions* (Chicago, University of Chicago Press, 1970).

16 Romans 12.2 (RSV).

17 See Kevin Eastell (ed.), *Appointed for Growth: A Handbook of Ministry Development and Appraisal* (London, Mowbray, 1994); and John White, *Changing on the Inside* (Guildford, Eagle, 1991).

18 As the context in John 8 makes clear, this is not a slogan for free-thinkers, but advice on discipleship and obedience.

19 Genesis 3.4–5.

20 St Gregory the Great, *Pastoral Care*, trans. Henry Davis (New York, Paulist Press, 1950).

21 James Campbell, *The Anglo-Saxons* (Oxford, Phaidon, 1982).

22 Bede, *Ecclesiastical History*, IV, 5 (Harmondsworth, Penguin, 1955).

23 Adapting the vision of John Tiller, *A Strategy for the Church's Ministry* (London, CIO, 1983).

24 Mark 7.13 (RSV): 'thus making void the word of God through your tradition'.

25 2 Corinthians 11.27–8 (RSV).

26 Russ Parker, *Free to Fail* (London, SPCK, 1992).

27 Colossians 1.24 ff.

28 George Herbert, 'The Church Porch' (1633), st. 56 (London, Penguin, 1991).

II BEING A PASTOR

1 Dietrich Bonhoeffer, *Life Together* (London, SCM Press, 1954), p. 87.
2 Ezekiel 34.3–16.
3 John 10.1–30.
4 Luke 10.25–37; see J. Court and K. Court, *The New Testament World* (Englewood Cliffs, NJ, Prentice-Hall, 1990), p. 172.
5 John 17.26 (NRSV).
6 John 21.15–19.
7 1 Peter 5.2–4 (RSV).
8 John Chrysostom, *On the Priesthood*, quoted in D. Tidball, *Skilful Shepherds* (Leicester, IVP, 1988), p. 155.
9 Exodus 18.18–23.
10 Ezekiel 3.3 (RSV).
11 John 21.15 (RSV).
12 e.g. Ephesians 4.11.
13 Hebrews 5.12–13 (NRSV).
14 1 Corinthians 3.9.
15 2 Corinthians 3.3.
16 Galatians 4.19.
17 Colossians 1.28.
18 Ephesians 4.15.
19 Eugene H. Peterson, *Under the Unpredictable Plant* (Grand Rapids, MI, Eerdmans, 1994), p. 87.
20 See Chapter 7 for visiting the parish in groups.
21 Richard Baxter, *The Reformed Pastor* (first edition 1656) (London, Banner of Truth, 1974).
22 For a more detailed review of the arguments, see Colin Buchanan, *A Case for Infant Baptism* (Nottingham, Grove, 1984), and Michael Green, *Baptism* (London, Hodder, 1987).
23 Isaiah 11.2.
24 Christopher Moody, *Eccentric Ministry* (London, Darton, Longman & Todd, 1992), ch. 8.
25 John Snow, *The Impossible Vocation: Ministry in the Mean Time* (Cambridge, MA, Cowley Publications, 1988).
26 Francis Bridger and David Atkinson, *Counselling in Context* (HarperCollins, London, 1994).
27 J. H. Oldham, *Florence Allshorn and the Story of St Julian's* (Coolham, St Julian's, 1990), pp. 27–8.

28 A. R. Day, *St Julian's 1941–1986* (Coolham, St Julian's, 1986), p. 4.

29 Henri Nouwen, *The Return of the Prodigal Son* (London, Darton, Longman & Todd, 1992).

30 *A Time to Heal*, a report for the House of Bishops (London, Church House Publishing, 2000), addresses the topics of both healing and deliverance.

31 Vincent J. Donovan, *Christianity Rediscovered* (London, SCM Press, 1978); Roland Allen, *Missionary Methods: St Paul's or Ours?* (London, World Dominion Press, 1912).

32 John 12.24 (NRSV).